THE MYSTERY OF
BARBARA FRITCHIE

★ A TRUE PATRIOT ★

The Mysteries of Barbara Fritchie

Did Barbara have a child? Was she an abolitionist? Was she a true patriot who waved the flag as depicted in John Greenleaf Whittier's famous poem? Read about the results of years of research on these questions by the author, Tamara Thayer, who is Barbara's fourth great-granddaughter.

Tamara Louise Thayer

The Fourth Great-Granddaughter of Barbara Fritchie

ISBN: 978-0-578-68321-8

Published by Minnesota Historical Writers

Printed in the United States of America
by Corporate Graphics, North Mankato, MN

First Edition

Final Copy Editor: Ellen Bisping

Photo Credits:
Author's photo of Barbara Fritchie was enhanced by Michael Sellner

Map by David Allen

Two photos are used with permission by the Historical Society of Frederick County and the Frederick Historical Museum. One photo taken by
Brad Sawyer is used with his permission. All other photos were taken by
the author or are no longer copyright protected.

Interior Design and Cover Design by Michael Sellner

Endorsements: Ellen Bisping, David Allen, and Thomas P. Ostrom

Dedication

**I dedicate this book to the patriotic memory of my
great great great great grandmother, Barbara Fritchie**

Completing this research would not have been possible without
the encouragement and patience of my family:

My mother, Edna Thayer, who traveled with me to Frederick, Maryland,
and to Oneida, New York, to explore the mysteries of Barbara

And to my late father, Dave Thayer, who always believed in his
lineage from Barbara and entrusted to me the one photo he had of her

My three children
Allison, Andrew, and Andrea

My three grandchildren
Brennan, Jackson, and Ireland

Acknowledgements

Special appreciation to the following individuals for their contributions to this book:

I'm grateful to my mother **Edna Thayer** for sharing the poem she wrote about Albert Augustus Thayer. Heartfelt thanks to her, as a fellow author, for her input along this journey, and accompanying me on two trips to Frederick, Maryland, to complete my research.

My gratitude to **Ellen Bisping**, the copy editor, for editing and writing her endorsement of the book. As both my former English teacher and a member of my church, she inspired my love of literature.

I deeply appreciate the invaluable contributions of **Michael Sellner**, designer, for his hard work with the layout and cover design. Michael Sellner won the 1st place 2014 CIPA EVVY Award for Interior Design and Layout for my first book, *A Country Doctor Goes To War*.

I am so grateful to **Andrew Cooney**, guest author, veteran, and a history buff for giving us a different perspective on Stonewall Jackson.

A special thank you to both **Dave Allen** and **Tom Ostrom** for their support in endorsing the book. All three of us have enjoyed the Veterans Roundtable, WWII Roundtable, and Civil War Roundtable in Rochester, Minnesota, where we participated as members, program presenters, volunteers, and live history re-enactors. We have participated on the WWII Roundtable Board of Directors and as officers during our many years of friendship.

CONTENTS

iii   Dedication

iv   Acknowledgements

v   Table of Contents

vi-vii   John Greenleaf Whittier's Poem

1   Chapter 1   A Brief Synopsis of Barbara

7   Chapter 2   The Birth of Barbara Fritchie

13   Chapter 3   Witnessing the Birth of a New Nation, and a Friend of George Washington

25   Chapter 4   The Mystery of Barbara's Child

33   Chapter 5   Life in Frederick; Friend of Francis Scott Key, Married Life to John

53   Chapter 6   An Abolitionist

61   Chapter 7   A Nation Divided

67   Chapter 8   Taking a look at Stonewall Jackson from both points of view (written by guest author Andrew Cooney)

73   Chapter 9   Whittier Inspires The Union

79   Chapter 10   The Alleged Cover-up Begins

107   Chapter 11   Conspiracy Theory

126   Chapter 12   Clues From The Author to Solve the Mystery

135   Chapter 13   Barbara's Legacy Continues to Inspire Patriotism

143   Chapter 14   Patriotism and The Flag; Be Inspired!

APPENDIXES

158   Timeline

170   Barbara (Hauer) Fritchie's Descendants

179   Glossary

185   Bibliography

189   A Lesson Learned for Historians, Genealogists, and Newspaper Reporters

190   Classroom/Book Club Discussion Questions

191   Checking Your Vexillology. Are You a Vexillologist?

192   About the Author

Who is Barbara Fritchie and why is she Famous?

There is no better description of her noble deeds from that historic September morn, than what is described in the words of John Greenleaf Whittier

Barbara Frietchie
Poem by John Greenleaf Whittier

Up from the meadows rich with corn,
Clear in the cool September morn,

The clustered spires of Frederick stand
Green-walled by the hills of Maryland.

Round about them orchards sweep,
Apple and peach tree fruited deep,

Fair as the garden of the Lord
To the eyes of the famished rebel horde,

On that pleasant morn of the early fall
When Lee marched over the mountain-wall;

Over the mountains winding down,
Horse and foot, into Frederick town.

Forty flags with their silver stars,
Forty flags with their crimson bars,

Flapped in the morning wind: the sun
Of noon looked down, and saw not one.

Up rose old Barbara Frietchie then,
Bowed with her fourscore years and ten;

Bravest of all in Frederick town,
She took up the flag the men hauled down;

In her attic window the staff she set,
To show that one heart was loyal yet,

Up the street came the rebel tread,
Stonewall Jackson riding ahead.

Under his slouched hat left and right
He glanced; the old flag met his sight.

'Halt!' - the dust-brown ranks stood fast.
'Fire!' - out blazed the rifle-blast.

It shivered the window, pane and sash;
It rent the banner with seam and gash.

Quick, as it fell, from the broken staff
Dame Barbara snatched the silken scarf.

She leaned far out on the window-sill,
And shook it forth with a royal will.

'Shoot, if you must, this old gray head,
But spare your country's flag,' she said.

A shade of sadness, a blush of shame,
Over the face of the leader came;

The nobler nature within him stirred
To life at that woman's deed and word;

'Who touches a hair of yon gray head
Dies like a dog! March on!' he said.

All day long through Frederick street
Sounded the tread of marching feet:

All day long that free flag tost
Over the heads of the rebel host.

Ever its torn folds rose and fell
On the loyal winds that loved it well;

And through the hill-gaps sunset light
Shone over it with a warm good-night.

Barbara Frietchie's work is o'er,
And the Rebel rides on his raids no more.

Honor to her! and let a tear
Fall, for her sake, on Stonewalls' bier.

Over Barbara Frietchie's grave,
Flag of Freedom and Union, wave!

Peace and order and beauty draw
Round thy symbol of light and law;

And ever the stars above look down
On thy stars below in Frederick town!

John Greenleaf Whittier

Note: The differences in spelling Fritchie is not a spelling error. Barbara spelled her last name without the extra "e" but Whittier named his poem after the old German spelling of her husband's last name "Frietchie."

This picture of Barbara is from the authors collection of ancestry pictures passed down to her.

1

★ A BRIEF SYNOPSIS OF BARBARA ★

Barbara (Hauer) Fritchie, the Great Great Great Great grandma of the author was a true patriot who made her descendants proud. She lived in Frederick Town, Maryland, a small town known to be at the crossroads of history. It has been compared to a wagon wheel by several sources, putting Frederick Town in the middle of that wheel and with the spokes being the small roads and rivers literally passing through the town going out in every direction; it was the perfect location to be at the crossroads of the Civil War. (See the map on page 63.) During the Civil War era, there would be times when the Southern troops would be camped just outside of Frederick, such as September 5 - 10, 1862 before they headed off to battle such as the Battle of South Mountain on September 14, 1862. Other times, it would be the Northern troops that would camp outside of town a few miles in either direction, sending small groups of men to town to get fresh supplies while the rest remained at camp waiting their next orders and getting ready for their next battle. Several horrific, bloody battles happened within a short distance from Frederick making it a perfect location to set up temporary hospitals to care for the wounded from both the North and South. Barbara volunteered in these hospitals under the direction of Dorothea Dix. Maryland was a border state which did not quite have enough votes to secede from the union when they voted, and since they were needed to stay in the union, they were permitted to remain a slaveholding state. This town was at the heart of political debate; people proudly displayed their flags to show their loyalty and, much to their surprise, there would be an even number of Confederate flags to the number of flags for the Union. In his poem, John Greenleaf Whittier didn't just pick any number to emphasize an even number of flags waving from both sides, however. As a Quaker and a very religious man, he would know the significance of the number 40 as it is used in the Bible. God's use of the number 40 is associated with judgement, testing, and times of trial. Whittier's use of the number 40 in his poem emphasizes the times of trouble or hardship with the Civil War.

Early on that September morning, Barbara heard several of the soldiers from Jackson's troops just outside her bedroom window as they were riding through town excited and full of mischief ripping down all the Union flags and leaving only the Confederate flags to wave. Barbara saw this and quickly went outside to pick up her flag that had been torn down and went back upstairs to her bedroom. She opened her window facing the river that the men had followed into town. She waved her flag at them proudly to show she was not going to let the Confederates get away with tearing it down. Jackson, seeing what was going on yelled the command, "Halt!" and then, "Fire!" One of the men aimed his rifle at her and shot with the bullet tearing the flag as it pierced her window frame. She was disgusted that this war was a threat to the unity of her country that she loved. She did not want to see it divided into two separate countries. By waving the flag at them, she was trying to make the point that they had only one true flag representing this country. This fear of seeing a divided country along with her pride in her flag was far greater than the fear of dying. She mustered up her bravery and, as stated in Whittier's poem, she did not back down to them.

'Shoot, if you must, this old gray head,
But spare your country's flag!' she said.

Jackson admired her feisty attitude and loyalty (and maybe he thought a poor elderly old woman was no threat to his cause, or maybe she reminded him of his own grandmother) but for whatever reason, he replied,

'Who touches a hair of yon gray head
Dies like a dog! March on!' he said.

In this quick response in that very moment, maybe he separated himself from the fearless ruthless general and acted as any gentleman would with compassion as he spared an old woman from an unnecessary death.

The author remembers with pride hearing her grandparents tell this very story of their brave ancestor Barbara Fritchie and how she stood up to Stonewall Jackson and his men. Barbara would rather risk her life than want the flag to fall in the hands of the Confederates who had been putting on a show of dragging their captured flags behind their horses or just throwing them to the ground in disrespect. One of the soldiers tore down a flag of the Union and tied it around one of his spurs as he rode through Frederick, Maryland. Some had personally kept the captured flags as trophies. It is similar to the winning regiment in a battle trying to capture the flag of the other regiment to show their victory. Barbara was not about to let her flag fall prey to this disrespect.

There was never a doubt by the author's family of the validity of Barbara's flag waving actions standing up to Stonewall Jackson and his men, and they were quite proud to be her descendants. They were filled with pride because Barbara was an abolitionist and outspoken against slavery. This story has been passed down enthusiastically and proudly through the generations.

The author's grandparents would also tell other stories of Barbara's patriotism. When she was younger, she met George Washington who, although being 34 years older became her friend long before he became a general and certainly even longer before he became the President of the United States. Washington had many good friends from Frederick Town including Thomas Johnson about whom you will read later. Washington gave Barbara a tea set and several years later he gave her a serving bowl. Barbara also was a great friend of Francis Scott Key who was the same age as her husband. The grandmother of the author said Barbara had received gifts from Key during their friendship, but her grandmother did not know whatever happened to those gifts or the tea set from George Washington.

Barbara's fascinating life included an inspirational display of patriotism. But Barbara had no idea that the poem Whittier wrote about her after her death would make her so famous. She also could not have foreseen the controversy and debate that would continue to this day regarding her actions. In the chapters to follow, several mysteries that still remain today about Barbara will be explained as you have never heard in any other publication about her life story.

Confederates occupied Frederick, Maryland

This picture was used on the Barbara Fritchie boxes of chocolates that were made in her honor.

2

★ THE BIRTH OF BARBARA FRITCHIE ★

Barbara's life story begged to be written from the moment it was discovered that there was so much effort to contradict her legend, which seemed like a conspiracy to debunk the famous life of Barbara. But why was it so important for so many in even her own beloved community to cast such doubt on a woman's noble actions after she was no longer alive to defend herself? This required deeper research into the biases of those with opposite points of view and what motives they had to support or discredit her actions. The author had to find out, knowing very well that her research may well lead in either direction proving or disproving Barbara's story. Within these pages, she presents to you Barbara's real story, starting from her beginning.

Johann Nicklaus Hauer was born August 6, 1733, in Diedendorf, Germany. Diedendorf is on the Saar in Lorraine between Strasbourg and Saarbrucken, also known as being between Saar-Union to the north and Fenetrange to the south. He immigrated from Diedendorf, Germany, on May 11, 1754, on board the "Neptune" arriving in Philadelphia, Pennsylvania, on October 1, 1754, and settling near Lancaster, Pennsylvania. He continued in Lancaster his skilled trade as a prominent hat maker. Catharine Ziegler was born in 1740 also in Germany. She married Johann in 1760 in Lancaster, Pennsylvania.

They lived in an area where many German immigrants were settling. This area is now known as the Pennsylvania Dutch area because it originally was so heavily populated by German immigrants. While keeping their former culture, they merged with a new Americanized culture forming a very unique population of Pennsylvania Dutch ethnicity, language, traditions, and culture, which is beautifully and uniquely their own.

Johann and Catharine had 10 children, of which their 5th child was Barbara Hauer, the subject of this story. (Some sources state that she was the 4th of eight children. There are two siblings who didn't live long and account for the difference in total number of siblings recorded). Barbara was born December 3, 1766, in Lancaster. She was just eleven days old when her family and sponsor Barbara Gamber had her baptized on December 14, 1766, by Rev. William Hendel in the First Reformed Church in Lancaster. She lived in an area where the German population was growing quickly. By 1790 there were about 100,000 Germans who had immigrated to America. This made up about 8.6 % of the total population. In 1790 in Pennsylvania, the German people represented 33% of the population compared to Maryland where it was only 12% of the total population. Prior to this time period, many German Protestants fled Germany to avoid religious persecution and were received by the English Sovereign and then sent as English colonists to early America.

At the time Barbara was born, the English colonies had been living under England's laws for 146 years, and people were tired of the taxation without representation and other issues. Barbara would have heard the constant political discussions, debates, uproars, and fights that led to the talk of declaring independence from England. The Declaration of Independence and the first flag for the new country came on July 4, 1776, when Barbara was just ten years old.[1]

Not much is known about Barbara during these early years except that she completed her education in Baltimore, Maryland. Julia Abbott, her grand-niece, stated that, "her education was the best that could be obtained in her day. She was not only able to read and write, but was a thoroughly well-read woman and was able to attend to her own business matters and sign her own business papers."

In her long lifetime, Barbara witnessed the creation of a nation as laws were established, new territories were added as states, an official flag (that would be ever-changing over the years) was developed, and amendments to the original constitution were made.

| 1736-1753 | 1753-1852 | 1853 - present |

The First Reformed Church in Lancaster was founded in 1721 using houses for the meeting place of German and Swiss settlers. The 2nd picture is of the church where Barabra was baptized in 1766. The third picture of the trio shows a church that was never attended by Barbara because she had already moved away from Lancaster by the time it was built, but it shows how her previous church looked in 1853.

---

[1] Some sources say she was about 10 years old when her parents moved from Lancaster, Pennsylvania, to Frederick, Maryland. *The Biographical Annals of Lancaster County, Pennsylvania: containing biographical and genealogical sketches of prominent and representative citizens and of many of the early settlers.* Chicago: J.H. Beers & Co., 1903, is one source that states they removed in 1770 to Frederick Town (now Frederick), MD (when she would have been just four years old). That same source, however, has several mistakes such as the spelling of both her mother's maiden name, and the pastor's name, as well as an incorrect marriage date for her. Another source says she moved "before 1783" which is anytime before she would have been 17 years old. The church records in Frederick indicate the Hauer family moved sometime in 1771 to Frederick, Maryland, when she was about five. (Nicolas set up his business which would be continued by a son and grandson.) One source for her brother Daniel Hauer states he was born in Lancaster County, PA in 1768 and about 1790 located to Frederick City and engaged in the manufacture of hats. Unless he moved to Frederick at a different time than the rest of his family, that would make Barbara much older when the family first arrived in Frederick.

Pictured here is the church that Barbara first attended in Frederick, Maryland, which is still standing today. This photo was taken in 2017 of the church originally known as the German Reformed Church, which became the Evangelical Reformed Church, United Church of Christ, of Frederick, Maryland. It has one of the many spires that were mentioned in Whittier's poem, and it is the oldest of the "Clustered Spires of Frederick". A new church was built for the congregation across the street at 15 West Church Street, but the church continued to keep and maintain both buildings. The Hauer family attended this same church.

On Good Friday, March 28, 1782, Barbara confirmed her faith as a member of the German Reformed Church. Then, as was tradition in her congregation in those days, after she had her Confirmation on Good Friday, it was followed by 1st Communion on Easter Sunday, March 30, 1782, by the pastor, Reverend Frederick Lewis Henop. He was also the same Reverend who baptized Francis Scott Key in 1779. When Maryland was a British Colony, the Key family belonged to the Church of England, and in Frederick, the All Saints Episcopal Church was the official church. The rector, a Tory, was driven out and fled to England during the American Revolution which brought the Key family to the German Reformed Church.

Barbara was described as a very beautiful and social young woman. This silhouette was made of her when she was young.

11

George Washington

3

★ WITNESSING THE BIRTH OF A NEW NATION, AND A FRIEND ★ OF GEORGE WASHINGTON

When George Washington was a young man, he would have come to Frederick, Maryland, many times. During the French and Indian War, he was a major in the militia and later served as Aide-de-Camp to General Braddock. During the French and Indian War his rank varied as a volunteer under Braddock, later he became a brevet Brigadier General. He stayed in this cabin in Frederick while he served Braddock.

The first photo is from the Frederick Historical Society and used with their permission.

The first picture is labeled as the cabin where young George stayed in Frederick when he was the Aide-de-Camp to Braddock. The second picture is labeled as "George Washington's headquarters" used during the American Revolutionary War (photo on the right), located on West All Saints Street along Carol Creek in Frederick. In 1913, it was torn down, but this picture of it remains and the place is labeled on local maps. These two buildings look like they have the same layout, and the author thinks it is possible they are the same building. The author couldn't find any local historian at this time who knew if they are separate buildings in different locations or if Washington used his earlier cabin for his secret headquarters at a later time.

There was also a gathering place to meet supporters secretly in the Catoctin Mountains just on the edge of Frederick, Maryland. There was a house in those mountains where the men could get a meal and have a drink while they discussed politics. As a young woman, Barbara is rumored to have worked there. She would have loved to hear the latest on the decisions of the government. There is only hearsay testimony of a woman who claimed that she worked at the meeting place in the mountains with Barbara Fritchie and other women. The author noticed when trying to find its location that the current Camp David is in that area. During the Revolutionary War, Washington had many "headquarters" set up throughout the colonies where his men would gather locally and discuss politics, get recruits, and discuss war strategy. The one in Frederick was a plain, inconspicuous building meant to blend in and not be obvious to the British as to its purpose. Several states revealed their meeting places for Washington's headquarters after the war and have preserved them as historical landmarks.

Washington's friend Thomas Johnson (1732-1819) lived in Frederick and was the one who recommended George Washington for Commander in Chief. Thomas Johnson became the first elected governor of the State of Maryland and Associate Justice of the United States Supreme Court.

Is it possible that Barbara and George Washington were closer friends than what history has recorded? Let us look at the history of

George Washington's relationship with women. We know of several young girls that he charmed and liked in his young childhood or school days. People described him as a charmer, good looking, well-educated, and affluent. His first love, Sally Cary Fairfax, was married to his good friend, George William Fairfax, a Virginia planter of a large plantation. In a letter to her, he states his feelings toward her and that, although it was a forbidden love or one that could never be because of the circumstances, she deserved to know his feelings.[2] He often joined her for tea and discussed world events.

Washington married Martha Curtis who was his social equal and a beautiful and wealthy widow of a Virginian. Martha's children were from her first marriage. Martha and George had a deep mutual respect and devoted friendship. She would write letters to him in his absence during the war or when he was in his office in Philadelphia. The letters were always filled with admiration and respect but not the romance of an intimate marriage. At the time it was not uncommon for people to marry for convenience or to enhance their social status. He was a loving husband, devoted father, and attentive grandfather to his stepchildren and grandchildren. We cannot assume that because they did not have children together that he was infertile. Childbirth was a difficult process back then, and many women died during the labor, and some became unable to bear a future child after a problematic delivery. Is it possible that Martha was not able to bear more children?

During his presidency, Washington had an office in Philadelphia, far from his home in Mount Vernon. It is here that he had a well-known relationship with Mrs. Powel. He enjoyed discussing politics over tea with her. He enjoyed conversations with headstrong well-educated women. She was married, and at times, the two couples

---

[2] founders.archives.gov contains several letters from George Washington to Sally Cary Fairfax including *From George Washington to Sarah Cary Fairfax, 12 September 1758.*

attended events together. Mrs. Powel had three miscarriages. She became friends with Martha. When George Washington was in Philadelphia, he would escort Mrs. Powel alone to social events. After he lost the office of President to Adams, he cleaned out his office in Philadelphia. Mrs. Powel bought his writing desk from that office at cost. She found taped under the desk a small collection of letters from Martha to George. She wrote to George stating that she had bundled them together and sealed them without looking at them. He wrote her back, stating that if she had peeked she would have read that Martha's letters were filled with love and admiration for a deep friendship, but it was not an intimate or sensual one. The preserved romantic letters to both Mrs. Powel and Mrs. Mary Cary became public. Ironically, Martha destroyed most of the letters he had written her saying they were private and should be kept that way. Letters about his advice on love and marriage written to Martha's children and grandchildren were preserved because they held onto them. How many other women received correspondence from George in his lifetime or even at the same time he was corresponding in these two well-known relationships?

The story passed down through the author's family oral history is that George and Barbara were good friends and often debated and discussed politics over tea. She was headstrong and opinionated, the very kind of woman George would have liked. Barbara was also beautiful in her youth. The family oral history also said George gave Barbara a full tea set in memory of all the times they enjoyed each other's company over tea. In 2016, there was only a single cup and saucer on display in the Barbara Fritchie home and one in the museum that is labeled from President George Washington. It is unclear if the larger set has dwindled down to one surviving cup and saucer in each place or if that is all that was originally given to her. There is also a coffee pot on display that was hers and the one from which she served George Washington in 1791 at the hotel on his famous visit. She must have been a very interesting conversationalist on politics as we know she entertained many guests in this manner. She had a wonderful reputation for entertaining and serving her delicious tarts, pies, and pastries during tea time to guests. The museum confirmed that story with their display of some of the fancy ornate dough cutters she used when baking. She was later a very good friend of Francis Scott Key and they too discussed worldly affairs over tea. General Reno who was passing through Frederick on his way to battle, stopped at Barbara's home for tea and to write a letter home from her writing desk. Barbara also served him some of her homemade wine and pastries. Barbara must have been able to hold an intelligent conversation with these men, and she must have been an enjoyable friend or she would not have made such lasting friendships as was the case with George and Francis. It is interesting to note that age differences did not seem to matter among her acquaintances; George was 34 years older, and Francis and her husband were both 15 years younger than she. George was well acquainted with Barbara's family too. Barbara's older sister Catherine Hauer married Major Peter Mantz, who would become the aide-de-camp to General George Washington. Peter was the descendant of John Mantz who fled Germany during the 30 years war. Peter served with the Maryland Flying Camp during the Revolutionary War. Peter Mantz was an officer of the Continental Army, to whom at

---

[3] From founders.archives.gov is the following paragraph:
The Maryland flying camp troops that GW sent forward included three companies commanded by Maj. Peter Mantz from Col. Charles Greenberry Griffith's 1st Regiment and apparently three companies commanded by Maj. James Eden from Col. Thomas Ewing's 3d Regiment (see Extract of a Letter to a Gentleman in Annapolis, 17 Sept., in Force, *American Archives*, 5th ser., 2:370–71; William Beatty, Jr., to William Beatty, Sr., 18 Sept., in the *Historical Magazine*, 2d ser., 1 [1867], 147; and Johnston, Harlem Heights, 82, and note 1). There is no evidence that any troops from Col. William Richardson's 4th Regiment fought on 16 September. The New England reinforcements included the remainder of Nixon's brigade and Col. William Douglas's and Col. Paul Dudley Sargent's regiments (see John Gooch to Thomas Fayerweather, 23 Sept., in "Revolutionary Actors," 334–35; Joseph Hodgkins to Sarah Perkins Hodgkins, 30 Sept., in Wade and Lively, This Glorious Cause, 221–23; Martin, *Private Yankee Doodle*, 42–43; and the returns of Nixon's, Sargent's, and Douglas's brigades, in Force, *American Archives*, 5th ser., 3:721–28).

the end of the Revolution, George Washington offered a commission as a Brigadier General in the regular army.[3] It is known that George came to Frederick on many occasions to visit several friends. Several letters of correspondence from George to friends state that he was traveling to Frederick to visit friends and then on to Washington or the other way around. When coming from Washington, he was stopping in Frederick to visit friends on his way to the Catoctin Mountains, too. Was Barbara included as one of these friends?

In 1791 President George Washington again came to Fredrick, Maryland, and stayed in the hotel there. This visit on June 30, 1791, was his first "official visit" into Frederick as President of the United States, and he had a formal banquet at Kimball's Tavern. Barbara was among the young ladies invited to serve him supper. Later, he enjoyed visiting with Barbara over tea. She was 25, and he was 58, but the age difference didn't matter with this friendship and their mutual interest in politics. This is the event when George gave Barbara a fine bowl as a gift. Some sources say that he invited his dear friends locally to join him, and that included Barbara Hauer as his dinner guest, not one of the servers. Current historians say that Barbara was among several local girls that were asked to serve President Washington and his guests dinner. (However, if Barbara was one of many waitresses, why would he give only Barbara a thank you gift?) The following source is from Terril Record:

> Across the street from Kimball Tavern lived an attractive dark-haired girl named Barbara Hauer, afterward immortalized as Barbara Fritchie. She, any Fredericktonian will declare, assisted Mrs Kimball in entertaining the President by pouring coffee for him out of a blue Staffordshire coffee pot now proudly displayed in Frederick. Evidently the charming Barbara's personality was as vivid in those days as when, 70 odd years later, she became Fredericks brightest star, a stellar position which, justly or not,

she has held here since-for it is declared that the Lowestloft bowl that is exhibited beside the coffee pot was presented to her from the appreciative and courtly general.[4]

Yet another source says that Barbara Hauer reportedly had the finest set of Liverpool china in town and brought it to the Tavern for use in this dinner. She also brought her coffee pot. Because she served George Washington with her coffee pot, it is on display in Frederick today. She joined the distinguished list of guests who dined with the president. As a thank you, President George Washington gave her a bowl that is also on display in Frederick.

The Kimball Tavern and Inn from 1797 to 1806 was located on part of the site where the current Francis Scott Key Hotel was built. This was a starting and stopping point for the stagecoaches at the Tavern so famous people have stayed there including Andrew Jackson, John C Calhoun, and Henry Clay who stayed on their way from the West to Washington.[5]

Barbara's outgoing personality and love for entertaining guests would have made this a perfect location for her to work. She made her own unique blends of tea with home-grown herbs and spices from her garden as well as adding her own special recipes when serving her delicate homemade petit fours that were so ornately decorated. She was curious about the political affairs of the country and was very opinionated and outspoken. Although this was not typical for her time period as a woman, she was still admired for it. As a young woman, she was rumored to be a waitress in both a tavern in the Frederick area (which could be the Kimball Tavern mentioned above or another

---

[4] *Terril Record*, February 22, 1934. *Terril Record* is a newspaper from Terril, Iowa.
[5] *The News*, Frederick, Maryland, October 8, 1949.

tavern), and rumored to waitress in a place outside of Frederick in the Catoctin Mountains mentioned earlier.

Another patriot in Barbara's family was Barbara's uncle Daniel Hauer who attended Wittenberg college. This prestigious Lutheran college in Germany is famous for its professors, the religious reformers Martin Luther and Phillipp Melanchthon. It was in this town of Wittenberg that the Protestant Reformation started on October 31, 1517, when Martin Luther nailed his 95 theses to the wooden doors of the Castle Church. It was there at Wittenberg University that Daniel Hauer met his schoolmate the Barron Johann DeKalb. Barron DeKalb had recruited others to join him to come to America and help the colonists fight against the British. Together, Barron DeKalb and Daniel Hauer traveled on the same ship to immigrate to Philadelphia, Pennsylvania. Johann DeKalb was a Franconian-French military officer who served as a major general in the Continental Army and died fighting the British in the Battle of Camden during the American Revolutionary War. Barron DeKalb was a brave patriot dying for the Americans to have independence from England.

England had a lot of war debt following the French and Indian War fought between 1754 - 1763. In March of 1765, England planned to pay off the debt with a tax on paper[6], the official Stamp Act which was to begin on November 1, 1765. Frustration filled the colonists who felt they were taxed too much. Frederick County was in the heart of the conflict against the British rule. On November 23, 1765, twelve judges in Frederick County publicly refused to obey the Stamp Act. Frederick Town responded with a parade. As a wonderful act of mockery, they creatively put a copy of the act in a coffin and paraded

---

[6] The tax on paper was for all printed materials such as newspapers, playing cards, magazines, and legal documents. The tax had to be paid with British currency and not the Colonial paper money.

through town. (It was an effigy of the man who was hired by the British monarchy to collect the tax, as the only mourner of the court's action.) That coffin and the effigy were buried together near the gallows on the old courthouse lawn close to the current city hall. The evening ended with a celebration ball. The Repudiation Act was one of the first acts of rebellion against England's rule.

The first two battles of Lexington and Concord occurred on April 19, 1775. Then, in the spring of 1775, two military companies from Frederick County were among the first southern volunteers to report to Boston and join George Washington. The Catoctin Furnace just outside of Frederick made cast shell, shot, and other camp equipment, and local gunsmiths made muskets for the Continental Army. Barbara's home county of Frederick also produced many political leaders. Some of the political stars who came from this county during and after the Revolutionary war were Thomas Johnson, a delegate to the Continental Congress who became Maryland's first state governor; Charles Carroll who signed the Declaration of Independence; John Hanson, and Thomas Sim Lee, both of whom served in the Continental Congress after the Revolution; Roger B. Taney, a judge and relative of Francis Scott Key; and Barbara Fritchie.

Barbara's family was definitely on the winning side of the Revolution and were all very patriotic. What an exciting time it must have been for Barbara to experience the birth of a new nation.

Dr. Casper Freitchie was a successful doctor and well-liked in Frederick Town. He and his wife had four children. He served in the British army and risked his life to spy for England. If history had gone another way and England had won the war against the colonies, Casper would have been a hero. There may have been statues memorializing him as a beloved doctor, family man, and military man who served his country. Instead, England lost the war and, with the colonies winning their declaration of independence against England, the colonies are known as the Patriots and not the rebels. Therefore, Casper's actions are forever recorded as the villain and the traitor in this scenario. The author does not for a minute suggest that she wanted the war to have turned out any other way. She is a very happy American and patriot who is only pointing out that, as in any war, the winning side declares the heroes and the victors and how historians will record the victory. The losing side is forever recorded in history as the villain.

Casper was one of seven men arrested and tried for treason on July 25, 1781. After the trial, four had been pardoned, and three were sentenced to be hanged. Casper was executed in the courthouse yard in Frederick on August 17, 1781. Casper was only 36 when he died, leaving his wife Susanne to raise their four children alone. John Casper was only one year and two months old when his father died. It must have been hard growing up in a town where the people knew his father was hung for treason. He probably felt ashamed. His mother was a very strong woman and spoke up for her rights by going to court and asking the judge to give her family back their home and personal items taken after Casper was arrested for treason. The judge agreed that she and her children needed their house to live, and everything was returned to her. Her youngest son, John Casper, became a skilled glove-maker. (John Casper is the future husband of Barbara Fritchie). It is interesting to note that Casper used the traditional German spelling of his last name. Did his son John Casper Fritchie drop the extra "e" to Americanize it or to separate from his father? Although John and Barbara Fritchie did not use that spelling, Whittier chose to use the traditional German original spelling of their ancestral name in his poem. This may have been his attempt to rally up the large German population in the area to join the north in the Civil War. By the time Barbara and John married, John was a well respected member of their community, and he was a well-known glove-maker continuing his successful business until his death.

Resources show two different dates for the marriage of Barbara and John as either May 6 or 18, 1806. Barbara Hauer was 39 years and five months when she was married to John Casper Fritchie who was 25 years of age when Reverend Wagner married them at the German Reformed Church in Frederick. John continued a successful trade and business as a glover and merchant. They lived on West Patrick Street next to Carroll Creek. Their original home was much larger than the replica that stands today which was built at 2/3 scale. The glover's shop was on the west side of the house next to the creek, and it is said that John could throw the scraps he didn't need out the window into the creek. Barbara's large bedroom was on the second floor with two windows facing the creek and one window facing Patrick Street.

John eventually hired Henry Hanshaw as a junior partner in his business. Henry began courting Barbara's niece Catherine Stover, and they were married in 1825 and lived near Barbara and John.

A picture of Barbara (Fritchie) Colburn, wife of Daniel Colburn. Her mother bent this tin type picture in half of the one she disowned.

4

★ THE MYSTERY OF BARBARA'S CHILD ★

The Barbara Fritchie Wikipedia page stated that Barbara was childless. The author was surprised to find out that the Wikipedia page was written by one person, a local Frederick historian, and was not a collaboration. He based this belief on the fact that Barbara was 39 when she married John Casper Fritchie, and he *assumed* that she was too old to bear children. The local historian however had no information on Barbara from the time of her baptism to her marriage to John. That Wikipedia page has been updated to no longer say she was childless. The author did come across a couple articles that also agreed she married past child-bearing years and, therefore, John and she never had children. In regard to the afore-mentioned comment about the age of childbirth, there are numerous family members on the author's family tree who have had children well into their 40's. For example, the author has a first cousin on her father's side who gave birth to her first child in her 40's and her 7th child one week before her 50th birthday. She chose to establish her career as a doctor and surgeon first before starting her family. And by the way, this same first cousin is also a biological fourth great-granddaughter of Barbara Fritchie. The author's first cousin on her mother's side had a son when he was 30 and later divorced. He was blessed to remarry when he was 46 and be a father again at 50 when his second wife, at age 40, gave birth to her first biological child, a son. The brothers may be 20 years apart but seem very close. The author's great aunt Christine Geistfeld gave birth to her daughter Lynne in 1959 when she was 47 years old, and Lynne's father Martin was 51. Lynne was their 7th child. The author's great grandma Augusta Pauline (Schulz) Wilke was 48 and her great grandfather August Friedrich "Fred" Wilke was 60 when they had their 10th child, Frederick Gerhardt Wilke in 1922, born in Madelia, Minnesota. The list would be too long to name all the other examples of close relatives on the author's family tree that have given birth after the age of 39, the age of Barbara Fritchie when she married and the age at which she was doubted to be able to give birth. Doubted by a few local Frederick historians and a Frederick tour guide who argued that Barbara was simply too old to bear children of her own by marrying so late. In checking the U.S. DEPARTMENT OF HEALTH AND HUMAN SERVICES Centers for Disease Control and Prevention, National Center for Health Statistics, National Vital Statistics System online records can provide interesting details. In 2015, there were 754 babies born to mothers over 50 in America. While the rate of pregnancy and live births has decreased among teenagers, the rate of births for women ages 30 - 50 has increased. While giving birth at that age is less common, it certainly has always been possible.

Although the Thayer family has passed down the information that they were descendants of Barbara Fritchie, ironically, it was never said that they descended from John Fritchie. Maude Thayer, who was the family historian, wrote down in her research that Mary Colburn was the granddaughter of Barbara Fritchie. Typically, it would be written "Mary Colburn is the granddaughter of Barbara Fritchie and (the First and Last name of the father)." But there is no mention in her records to say who was the father of Barbara's child. Was she born from a previous marriage in which case, many times that was never discussed? Was she born out of wedlock in which case, the child would not have been allowed to be baptized in the Hauer's church, and that would explain why there are no baptismal records for Barbara's child in her home congregation. Also, an illegitimate child at that time would not have a birth certificate. In a later census report in John and Barbara's household, a little girl is listed. Some stories claimed that Barbara took in John's younger sibling because they were orphaned after the death of his father. However, all his siblings would have been older than him and, therefore, able to care for themselves by the time he married. They also would be much older than the girl in the census report. Barbara is rumored to have adopted a niece, too. Was Barbara's real daughter passed off as John's sibling or as her adopted niece? Barbara did take in a niece twice for a short time to help out the niece. Her niece Catherine Stover lived with Barbara and John for a short time before she married Henry, at which time she and Henry moved into their house near-by. In Barbara's last few years of life, she did take in another niece, Harriet Yoner. The author has not yet come across any records of Barbara adopting a niece as some sources from that time period state she had adopted and raised a niece. Based on the author's family history of having children into ones 40's, Barbara and John could have had a child together. Any of these theories are possibilities and worth investigating further. Only a DNA test could prove who is the father of Barbara's child. Even a birthdate is not known for Barbara Fritchie's daughter. It is not known if she was conceived from another earlier marriage about which no one knows, if she were conceived later by her husband John when she was 39, or if she was born out of wedlock before Barbara married John. Any of these scenarios are possible so a DNA match now could only be confirmed to Barbara herself or her Hauer family and may or may not match with descendants of John Fritchie. A DNA test might not match any of the Fritchie descendants from John's siblings since his parentage of Barbara's daughter is still unknown. The author is willing to do any requested DNA test with any Hauer descendants or from Barbara's DNA to prove that Barbara is the author's fourth great-grandmother. Note: on both 23andMe and on ancestry.com, the author has already done DNA testing. Several people match as 5th-8th cousins who share the last name of Hauer on both trees. One of the matches shows the "only" name that is shared on both trees is the Hauer name. Note that two of Barbara's siblings whose descendants moved to the midwest went by Howard and not Hauer.

These matches are found on my ancestry.com DNA results page. It is interesting to note that there are no matches between the author and the last name of Fritchie. Perhaps none of them have taken the test or more likely there is no connection.

Just looking at the profiles of the author's father and that of Barbara Fritchie, one can see a real family resemblance.

In John's diary, he states how grateful he is to Barbara for all the support they have given each other over the years, and his life was better for knowing her. It is unclear exactly to what he is referring, but the author believes that when John married Barbara, she improved his social standing after the embarrassment of his father's death for treason. If she had a child before their marriage, then the marriage would legitimize that child. The marriage may have served a double purpose for both of them.

The Thayer's family story from oral and written history is that Barbara Fritchie had a daughter also named Barbara Fritchie. There was a coachman, Daniel Colburn, passing through town recruiting young converts to the new Oneida Community located in Oneida, New York. This was a new religious sect headed by Rev. John Noyes that believed in perfectionism and believed in communal sharing of everything. They were a very strict religious group with daily religion study but also practiced free love as part of their communal beliefs. Barbara Hauer Fritchie told her daughter that if she ran away with the coachman, she would be disowned. Barbara (the daughter) did run away with Daniel Colburn and headed for Oneida, New York. Barbara kept her word and disowned her daughter. Little is known about what Daniel and the daughter did once they arrived in Oneida. They may or may not have joined the commune. They may have lived in the town or surrounding area instead. The Oneida Community employed some people from the neighboring communities as well.

In 2016, the author and her mother went to stay at the Oneida Community Mansion to search their wonderful records. It was a very interesting museum and the grounds are well preserved. They do have more than one Barbara listed without last names in their roster. One "Barbara" matched as a possibility with a child named Mary, but again, no last names were listed. They do list Daniel Colburn.

It is known that the Daniel and Barbara on my family tree had a daughter Mary Colburn born in Oneida, New York. This Mary Colburn is my great great grandmother. It is not known if Mary had any siblings or was an only child. One source said she has a brother Will Colburn that traveled with her to Minnesota. Some sources state she is born near Corning, New York, and other sources listed her place of birth as in Oneida, New York. There are many Colburn families during this time period from both Corning and Oneida.

A picture of the Oneida Community.
(It is unknown if Barbara Colburn is among them)

President Lincoln thought the Oneida Community practice and several other radical new religious sects around the country of the time were immoral so he put pressure on them to close down and disband. The Oneida Community felt it was hard to disband and go their separate ways when they were all family. They decided to continue their business practices that had supported them all those years and form the Oneida Ltd Company. The company continued to make several products such as animal traps, and the fine Oneida silverware for which they were famous. Many then stayed in the surrounding area close to family and worked for the company.

After the Civil War in 1865, the United States government was financially depleted with the reconstruction period and was not able to pay all the pensions to the veterans from the war, so many Civil War veterans were given 180 acres of free land in the new state of Minnesota and other midwest states as their pension. The population of wounded veterans needing care was great in Minnesota and its citizens built soldiers homes to care for veterans.

After the war, Mary Colburn, the granddaughter of Barbara Fritchie, was married to Albert Augustus Thayer, a former drummer boy in the Minnesota 7th Regiment, company C. A brief glimpse of their two children can be found in the Appendix under "Barbara (Hauer) Fritchie's Descendants."

CHINA-WARE
the property of
BARBARA FRITCHIE

Barbara Fritchie's China

5

★ LIFE IN FREDERICK; FRIEND OF FRANCIS SCOTT KEY, MARRIED LIFE TO JOHN ★

Barbara and John were well-respected in Frederick, Maryland. John was a skilled glove maker. Barbara was social and loved to entertain with tea, coffee, or her homemade wine, and her homemade fine delicacies consisting of ornate petite pastries, cookies, pies, etc. She spent hours tending to her garden and the many flowers she planted around her house.

Barbara's niece Catherine Hauer married Jacob Byerly who was the son of the Frederick photographer. While his father specialized in the daguerreotype photos, Jacob Byerly specialized in the new tin type. They took Barbara's photo several times to prepare for the Great Fair. It was the trending practice of photographers to have women use wigs, or put black shoe polish on their hair to make them look younger. Both the photo the author has which Barbara gave to her granddaughter and another that is in the Frederick Museum at 24 Church Street are of Barbara with grey hair. She has a fuller face in these two pictures so they are probably taken in her late 80's or early 90's. The photo that is used most often around Frederick of her is with very black hair. Her face is thinner, her hair line has receded, and there are more wrinkles in her face indicating she is much older than this picture indicates. It is misleading because the older picture of her shows the black hair, and the younger picture is when she is grey. Byerly probably just wanted her to demonstrate this for the Great Fair where he had his photo booth set up. When the author was in the office of the same local Frederick historian with whom she had been corresponding for research several years ago, trying to explain her connection to Barbara, he received an email from Brad Sawyer who was pricing Civil War pictures for an auction house. In this collection was a picture of Barbara that was labeled "Barbara Fritchie". Brad had asked this historian in his email if it was authentic. The historian in his reply said that there is "only one authentic picture of Barbara" and that is the one they use of her with the dark hair. He said they were lucky to have the one they have of her and did not think, with her financial means, she would have had more than one taken. How can other pictures of her be dismissed without investigation or having an expert look at the facial similarities? Of course with a photographer in the family, Barbara probably would have had many taken. One negative of a glass template of yet another pose in the museum artifacts says the original photo was given to her descendants. In that picture she has grey hair, and it is of a 3rd pose, not the one the author has and not the one in this chapter. Are there others who own pictures of Barbara and have been told they are not authentic?

This picture is used with permission by Brad Sawyer. The actual photo has been purchased by the author.

The picture on the left is located at the Frederick County Historical Museum at 24 Church Street, Frederick, MD and is used with their permission. The painting on the right was hanging in the Barbara Fritchie home.

There are also a few paintings of Barbara Fritchie showing the flag waving incident, and one is of a portrait of her. The portrait was hanging on the wall of her home when it was a public museum. When the author asked the source of that portrait, it was unknown. That portrait is no longer at the Barbara Fritchie AirBnB, and its location is unknown. Notice how much the portrait of the younger Barbara has a fuller face and resembles the author's photo of Barbara. The author will display on her book website any other pictures that are labeled as or believed to be of Barbara Fritchie, but the owners of them were told that they are not authentic. It would be interesting to have a photo expert compare them.

What was Barbara's "financial means" as this historian implied she was poor and unable to afford more than one photo of herself? She inherited money from her parents as mentioned in their will. Her husband made a good living. She sold items she knitted. They owned a few properties in town from which they collected rent for a steady additional income. There are court records from John taking one renter to court for rent owed on one of his houses. Barbara asked a church member for advice on investing money and, in following his advice, it is reported that she profited. She inherited money in her husband's will. The original house Barbara and John lived in is the comparable size house to the homes of Judge Taney, Francis Scott Key, or other prominent locals from that time period.[7] Her favorite dress was made of expensive purple silk and had fine detail. It is the author's opinion that Barbara had financial means to live a comfortable life and afford multiple pictures of herself.

Barbara's father Nicholas Hauer died in Frederick on December 7, 1799, at only 66 years old. Her family buried him in the church

---

[7] The replica house one can see today in Frederick was built at 2/3 scale farther away from the creek that had flooded her previous home.

cemetery at the German Reformed Church. Then just seven days later, she lost her good friend George Washington.

President Washington died at only 67 years old on December 14, 1799, at his home in Mount Vernon. He had an acute epiglottitis and died from its complications. Barbara was 37 at the time of his death. Barbara Hauer and Francis Scott Key planned the public memorial service for President George Washington.

A Friend of Francis Scott Key

Barbara was a very good friend of Francis Scott Key, and they enjoyed their conversations about politics over tea. Francis Scott Key grew up in Frederick and became a lawyer, poet, and author. They seemed like the perfect pair to plan President George Washington's memorial. Francis and his brother-in-law shared a law office in Frederick. His brother-in-law became the famous judge who made the awful Dred Scott ruling that was so criticized. In 1812 Francis went to Boston to negotiate the release of some of U.S. citizens held prisoner on the English ship. He witnessed the bombardment of his homeland under attack. He would have shared this story with Barbara and his relief to see the American flag still waving when he decided to write a poem about that experience. This poem became our national anthem, "The Star Spangled Banner." On August 24, 1825, Francis delivered an address in Barbara's church. Barbara's abolitionist beliefs encouraged Key to give his slaves their freedom. This was his metanoia experience[8] in which by 1830, all of Francis Scott Keys slaves were free. He hired one of his former slaves to be his foreman. Francis started to represent black slaves who had earned their freedom but were not granted it by their owners. Francis would represent

---

[8] The experience of abandoning an old conditioned self, learned behavior or beliefs for a more open-minded, educated, self-awareness, global understanding and acceptance of all humanity. The moment of change from the inner core outward in ones beliefs.

people who were black to make sure justice was equal for everyone. However, when one person who was black was guilty of a crime and Francis was on the prosecuting end of the trial, it did not go over well with the black community.

Francis moved to Washington DC where he held many important positions. Francis returned often to Frederick which was a short distance from Washington DC to visit his family and friends. Barbara always enjoyed getting the latest news on what was happening in our country. They were life-long friends, and Francis gave Barbara a shawl for a gift; it is on display in Frederick.

The memorial for Francis Scott Key at the Mount Olivet Cemetery.

Married life to John

Barbara and John were a very active part of their community. Their home on Patrick Street was in an appealing location in the business section of town which was good for his business, and they lived alongside the beautiful, charming, and scenic creek. They had their name on their family pew in church reserving their seat for worship. They were outspoken abolitionists who tried to convince slave owners to free their slaves. They believed God created all people equal. They both had many family members who lived in Frederick.

Jacob Engelbrecht ('en-gəl-, bre<u>k</u>t), lived across the street from John and Barbara Fritchie on Patrick Street. His father had been a Hessian prisoner in the barracks in Frederick during the American Revolutionary War. After the war he stayed in Frederick. Jacob wrote a couple entries a week for years in a diary which has become a wonderful resource for the historians in Frederick. Even though, of course, he did not write down every major event, he did an excellent job recording what he could.

This excerpt is from Jacob's diary:

On Sept 16, 1841 Barbara's brother, Daniel Hauer died at 74 years old. He was from Frederick and brother to: Henry, Barbara, Mrs Stover, Mrs Peter Mantz, and the late Mrs Jacob Steiner and the father of Mr. Nicolas D Hauer. He was buried in the German Reformed graveyard in Frederick, MD.

You can see from that simple entry in his diary how genealogists or historians can get a lot of valuable information. The only problem is some of his entries are filled with his biased opinions and comments typical of a "diary" and not that of an unbiased account of historical events.

Barbara and John were happily married for 43 1/2 years until John passed away on November 9, 1849. He became ill earlier in 1849 and purchased a burial plot in the German Reform Church Cemetery. Henry Henshaw continued his glove business from the Fritchie home.

The Widow Meets Her Granddaughter For The First Time

Again, no one knows for sure if Daniel, Barbara, and Mary were ever living in the actual Onieda commune or not. It was around 1856 that Mary Colburn left her parents and traveled to Frederick, Maryland, to meet her grandmother. Barbara Fritchie gave Mary a picture of herself and Mary gave her grandmother a picture of her mother which Barbara bent in half. There is no way of knowing how Barbara felt about her granddaughter. No one knows what Barbara told Mary about her mother and her version of why she disowned her. After their visit, Mary returned to Oneida, New York, where Mary joined a group of settlers traveling in covered wagons headed west. In this group were the Noyes family who were from Maine and happened to be cousins of the Noyes who started the Oneida Community. They settled in the Fair Haven Township, Stearns County, of the Minnesota Territory. The Noyes family from Maine were members of the Baptist denomination and were very faithful brethren. Mary Colburn found herself in a new territory full of new beginnings.

Minnesota became a territory on March 3, 1849, and soon many settlers arrived. There had been a lot of incentives to encourage new settlers to come to this growing territory in hopes of making it another state for the union. One incentive was to earn free land with "The Homestead Act." If one can homestead and show land improvement for five years the land was theirs. The railroads were joining the East Coast to the West Coast requiring opportunities for new employment along the route. The new clothing fashion of the black top hats made of beaver hide was drawing trappers to come to the Minnesota Territory to supply most of the beaver and other furs used in the East Coast and in England. Minnesota became the 32nd state on May 11, 1858, created from just the Eastern part in the original Minnesota Territory.

Mary Colburn would have experienced this exciting growth period in Minnesota as this beautiful scenic state was developed. She had settled there just two years before it became a state. It is unknown how many times she was able to go to Frederick, Maryland, to see her grandmother or if the one time mentioned earlier was her only time.

An excerpt from Jacob's diary:

> 95 years - This day Mrs. **Barbara Fritchie** widow of the late John Casper is 95 years old. She was born "December 3, 1766". She lives opposite our residence at the Bentztown Bridge **and is very active for a person of her age**. Tuesday December 3d 1861. 11 o'clock AM.[9]

---

[9] Note: the author left this date exactly how Jacob wrote it out in his diary instead of adding the commas and removing the d after the 3 indicating the third.

Barbara made her will in March of 1862:

<u>In the Name of God Amen.</u>

<u>I Barbara Fritchie</u> of Frederick City, in Frederick County in the state of Maryland, being in ordinary health of body, and of Sound and disposing Mind, Memory and understanding, do make and publish, this my Last will and Testament in Manner and form following,

<u>First</u> and principally, I commit my body to the earth, and my immortal Soul to God, who gave it, in humble reliance on the atoning merits of Jesus Christ, "My Saviour, and direct that my hereinafter named Executor, shall have me decently buried, and after my said Executor shall have paid all my debts and funeral expenses and deducted ten per cent commissions for his trouble in settling up my Estate. I then give devise and bequeath as follows,

<u>1st Item</u>, I do hereby give and bequeath to Mrs. Catherine Hanshaw, wife of Henry Hanshaw, and her heirs, all my household and kitchen furniture.

<u>2nd Item</u>, I do hereby give and bequeath to Mrs. Catharine Hanshaw afore said all my wearing apparel.

<u>3rd Item</u>, I do hereby give and bequeath to Mrs. Catharine Hanshaw afore said all my silver Plate,

<u>4th Item</u>, I do hereby give and bequeath to wife Henrietta Yoner, now residing with me, one hundred dollars, and also desire that she reside with Mrs. Catherine Hanshaw's family during her life or as long as she may think proper to remain with them.

<u>5th Item</u>, I do hereby give and bequeath to Mrs. Margaret Watkins my niece, the Sum of Sixty dollars.

<u>6th Item</u>, I do hereby give and bequeath to Wife Emily Hanshaw daughter of Henry Hanshaw, the Sum of Sixty dollars,

<u>7th Item</u>, I do hereby give and bequeath to my esteemed friend and Pastor the Rev. Daniel Zacharias, One hundred dollars,

<u>8th Item</u>, I hereby give, devise, and bequeath to Mrs. Catherine

Hanshaw wife of Henry Hanshaw, aforesaid, and her heirs all the cash and residue of my property, Real personal and Mixed.

And Lastly, I do nominate, constitute and appoint my nephew Nicholas D. Hauer, the Executor of this my Last Will and Testament evoking and acceeding all former wills, by me heretofore made ratifying and compromising this and none other to be My Last Will and Testament.

In Testimony whereof I have hereunto set my hand and affixing my seal this fourth day of March in the year of our Lord, Eighteen hundred and Sixty two.

Signed Sealed published and declared by Barbara Fritchie the above named Testator, as and for the last will and testament, in the presence of us, who at her request in her presence, and in the presence of each other have Subscribed our Named Thereto.

Barbara Fritchie's signature followed with her seal.   ~*~

Author's comments about this will:

Notice Barbara didn't bequeath the flag used in the famous flag waving incident because this Will was drawn up six months before it occurred.

She didn't leave anything to her only daughter because, of course, as mentioned earlier, her only child, Barbara Colburn, was already disowned and deceased.

It is important to point out that there is no mention of any slaves which is strong proof that Barbara didn't have any. If she did own any slaves, they would have to be mentioned as to what happens upon her death. She would have to bequeath any slaves to someone or give them their freedom. But there is NO mention of any in her will which is another form of proof that she didn't own slaves.

Barbara must have been worried as she was following the progress of the Civil War. The Confederates were moving toward Frederick the beginning of September, 1862, as General Lee started his Maryland Campaign.

From Jacob's diary:

> Commotion - this morning our town is in a small commotion. The report is that General Jackson has crossed the Potomac at Noland's Ferry (12 or 14 miles south of this place) with 12,000 men. The report also is that General Sigel of United States Army is near by. Also report that the Rebels have crossed the Potomac this side of Cumberland and many other reports on the same subject. Time will show. Another report says they had a **battle near** the Point of Rocks last evening **but we did not hear** any cannon firing at that time.
> Friday September 5, 1862 9 1/2 AM

Author's note: The time was kept how Jacob wrote it as 9 1/2 AM since it's a direct quote instead of changing it to 9:30 a.m.

This quote is from September 6, 1862 from Jacob's diary:

> Tremendous excitement "Jackson is coming" - Last night the report is that Jackson's Army (Rebel Army) were at Benjamin M Moffat's farm 3 miles below Buckstown on their way to Frederick. The Provost Marshall received a telegraph dispatch, that in the event of the enemy's approaching, to destroy the government stores. Accordingly about 10 o'clock they commenced burning beds & cots that were stored at "Kemp Hall" corner of Market and Church Street and burnt to the amount of about ___>. At the Barracks they burnt some stores also at the depot they burnt tents, cots, beds, guns, (muskets). Soldiers clothing and shoes were forgotten which fell into the Rebels hands. In all this **commotion, myself &**

wife heard nothing of it.
Saturday September 6, 1862, 8 o'clock AM

Is it possible that Jacob and his wife missed Stonewall and his men shooting at Barbara from the far side of her house? In his own words above, both he and his wife heard nothing of any "commotion" prior to 8:00 am. In that case, they would not have heard Barbara's confrontation with Jackson and his men earlier that same morning on September 6, 1862.

In the book *Barbara Fritchie, a Study*, by Caroline H. Dall, she writes:

> It was just before sunrise on Saturday, September 6, 1862, that the advance guard of Lee's army, under Stonewall Jackson, came down the Bentztown road. I do not mean that the advance entered Frederick, - it certainly did not; but Stonewall Jackson did. A little while before the troops came within sight of Barbara's window…[10]

Several diary entries from confederate soldiers who were there also wrote that it happened on September 6, 1862.

Jacob Engelbrecht wrote another entry in his diary on September 6:

> Frederick captured by the Rebels - This morning about 10 o'clock the Rebels took possession our good city of Frederik without opposition. No soldiers of the United States being here. About 5 or 6 thousand calvary and infantry & also 3 batteries of artillery (2 of 5 guns & 1 of 3 guns) (13 cannon) thus far there has been. No commotion, or excitement, but all peacefully and quiet. The soldiers are around town purchasing clothing, shoes, boots, caps & eatables. While I was at dinner

---

[10] *Barbara Fritchie, a Study*, by Carline H. Dall (1892), on page 38.

I am told about 7 more cannon went through town. Many of our citizens left town last night & this morning. The postmaster with all the mail matter and all officers of government appointment, telegraph &c put out.
Saturday September 6, 1862 1 o'clock PM

It sounds like the Confederate soldiers were all over town so why is it that people today deny that Stonewall or his men passed by Barbara's house and even deny they were in town? One historian and another author said that the only proven day that Stonewall's men marched through town was on September 10 based on a photograph they have of the Confederates marching through town. There are reasons why the date was September 6 and not the 10. First, there are records of Stonewall and his men going through Frederick many times but not on a "formal march". At no time does Whittier refer to "Jackson's men" as being the full regiment. It could have been just a few. Many times the regiment was camped just outside of town and several men would ride into town for the supplies. Secondly, Whittier never said what day in early September the flag incident happened so why are they picking the 10th themselves and trying so hard to prove it could have happened on that one and only day? Stonewall was there in Frederick so often between September 5 - 10, that the people of Frederick nicknamed the hitching post for Jackson's horse "Stonewall's Post". This post was outside his friend's home, Dr. Ross, the reverend of the Presbyterian church. And thirdly, the picture to which they make reference as the only existing picture of the rebel march through Frederick on September 10, has been in print many times with captions for different dates that the photo took place. Two historians wrote a lengthy article stating that, after examining the photo, they do not believe it was taken until toward the end of the war based on the guns used in the photo, and the shadowing from the sun indicates a different time of year. And lastly, another point about this is that Jacob Engelbrecht mentions further in his diary for the 6th that there were about 60,000 men camped around Frederick, two to three miles out. The town had been completely taken over by them. Many other reports are of people hearing gun shots in town from the excited rebels as they were going through town getting ready for their big battle which is now known as Lee's Maryland Campaign. People heard the gunshots and stayed inside their homes without going to the windows for their own safety. Others reported that the rebels went about town without incident shooting guns to try them out before purchase, and there was no fear by the people. It would depend on which side one's loyalties were. In any case, if people heard gun shots, they would not know if it were the incident Barbara experienced or the previously stated shots heard because people were staying inside for protection.

On the morning that Barbara confronted Stonewall Jackson, Engebrecht wrote that he did not hear any of the commotion. Some of the people who believe Barbara did not wave the flag use as their only proof that this Jacob did not record it in his diary. But he would not record it if he did not hear any commotion prior to 8:00am. He also did not record anything about the other two women who were witnessed to wave the flag after Barbara on different days in different situations and different locations. He could not have been at his window 24/7. He would have been asleep at sunrise when Barbara waved the flag. Several days each week, he made no entries in his diary at all. It would have been very loud outside during the night as reportedly people with Northern Union support moved out of town until the Confederate occupation was gone. According to Jacob and other resources, the local citizens were destroying and burning items right in the middle of the street that may have been useful to the Confederate soldiers. People stayed inside their homes and hunkered down afraid of any confrontation. It is not surprising that there were only a few witnesses to Barbara's ordeal and that Jacob slept through it.

Tamara Thayer portraying her fourth great-grandma Barbara from her dormer window.

Tamara is waving the flag from the bedroom window where she believes Barbara actually confronted the men.

Also from Jacob's window facing the street, he could not see Barbara's bedroom window facing the creek where the men rode into town. It has long been assumed that Barbara waved her flag out the front dormer bedroom window facing the street as the example in the picture shows.

The only hint of which window was used from Whittier is when he states in his poem that she waved the flag from her attic window. The top floor has two windows facing the street and two windows facing the creek. One facing the street is from another room. In all, she has three bedroom windows. The picture is showing the side of her house facing the creek and her bedroom has the top two windows. Both of the side windows give her an overlook up and down the creek the soldiers would have followed into town from their camp just two to three miles outside town. The Reverend Ross lived along this very creek as well. Her original house was much closer to the creek. The road in front of her house has changed since the Civil War, and the bridge just before her house was changed at the time the Creek was widened.

On September 8, Jacob said in his diary at least 10,000 confederates came to town to buy things in the stores. This was great financially for the local business owners who sold most of their inventory.

Word of Barbara's waving the flag in true patriotism toward

Jackson's men inspired many other women to do the same thing throughout the rest of the war. The author was told at first by the Frederick historian that Frederick had another woman, Mary Quantrill, just down the street from Barbara who waved the flag on September 10th and that she was the one who waved it, not Barbara. He has added historical landmarks and changed wording on other historical signage to declare that it was Mary and not Barbara who waved the flag. But if what he says is true that Mary waved the flag on the 10th, then the two women waved the flag on different days and so proving that Mary waved the flag does not disprove that Barbara waved it. So the author researched in depth Mary Quantrill's story as well.

Mary was born in Hagerstown and was living with her husband and children in Washington right before the war. Her husband worked for a paper in Washington and was getting criticized for his views on politics. He moved his children and wife to Frederick where they could live with Mary's mother during the war. Mary decided while living in her parents home she would homeschool three of her children and three other children of Southern Sympathizers. She is currently described by a local historian in Frederick as being a Unionist who grew up in Frederick and a long time school teacher in Frederick before the flag incident. He says that, as she waved the small union flag at the Confederates as they marched down Patrick Street on the 10th, it was taken from her so one of her students, Mary Hopwood, handed her another one. The census report, however, shows that she was still living in Washington with her family right before the war began, so she did not teach for long in Frederick before the flag incident. It also seems more likely that she had the same loyalties to the secession as her husband's uncle William Quantrill who formed the Quantrill Raiders. They were known as pro-Confederate partisan guerrillas. Members included the famous Jesse James and his brother Frank. They were responsible for the attack of Lawrence, Kansas later known as the Lawrence massacre. It seems unlikely to the author that Mary had any loyalties to the Union.

On October 1, 1862, President Lincoln and his Suite visited Frederick for a three-day stay as they visited the nearby battle fields.

The Civil War wounded throughout the war were brought into town to be cared for in several churches that were used as hospitals along with Kemp Hall.

The church basement was used as a makeshift hospital during the Civil War treating wounded soldiers as needed from both the Union and Confederacy. A tour guide explained that several of the churches on Church Street were used to house the many wounded soldiers from the several battles that took place close to Frederick.

This drawing is of the Second Presbyterian Church Hospital, Frederick City, Maryland. It is the typical look of how several of the churches accommodated the veterans and doctors. Barbara would help Dorothea Dix care for the wounded. She brought her homemade pastries for the soldiers to eat and visited with them. Like Dorothea Dix, they cared for both the Union and the Confederates. Barbara's own church just divided the basement into half for the Confederates on one side and the Union army on the other. Dorothea Dix admired Barbara's help.

Barbara celebrated her 96th birthday on December 3, 1862, with family and friends at a party in her home. She was enjoying her party with her homemade wine and birthday cake. She was very healthy according to the family and friends who attended. Her family said she became ill with a cold shortly after the party, and it developed into a pneumonia which caused her death just two weeks later. There were also rumors that when she waved the flag at Stonewall and his men that she caught her cold on that cool September morning. The author's opinion is that if she became sick that day and died three months later, she would not have been able to do all the volunteering in the hospital that took place in these same months or hosting her own birthday party if she already had pneumonia.

Barbara died December 18, 1862 at 6:00 pm, at 96 years and 15 days.

On October 1863, about 13 months after the incident of Barbara waving the flag, Whittier's poem was published. It gained world-wide fame.

A picture of her original house appeared on page 269 in the Harpers Weekly in the April 25, 1868, issue. The page showed three historic houses that were neglected and should be preserved for historic reasons. Barbara's house was one of the three.

The Barbara Fritchie house was sold to Mr James Hopwood who could not wait to tear it down and get rid of her legacy. He bought it for $300, and it was recorded in Engelbrecht's diary on April 3, 1869. He stated that Hopwood wanted to remove the house by the 15th of that month. James Hopwood's daughter was at Mary Quantril's when she waved a flag, and he was tired of the popularity and publicity that Barbara received. People all over the world wrote to the newspapers upset that the Barbara House was going to be destroyed. After it was removed, tourists still wanted to see where the house was, and so a sign was put up in the location where the house once stood.

Removing her house did not remove her legacy as some of the local Southern Sympathizers had hoped. Tourists still flocked to the area asking to hear her story and see the location where it all happened. Later it was decided that a replica house should be built at 2/3 scale of the original for tourists. It was built farther away from the creek but in the same general location. The house was a big tourist attraction. Family members put in the house some of her original furniture and possessions. One of her nieces moved into the house and ran the tours. Over the years, tourists could find in Frederick many souvenirs such as tea cups, candy, plates, etc. made to pay tribute to Barbara Fritchie.

This photo of one of the original postcards from Frederick is used by permission from the Frederick Historical Museum.

The author and her mother enjoyed a wonderful tour of both buildings when they were in Frederick in 2016. The author returned with a friend in 2017 and gathered more information. Her third visit for research on Barbara took place in 2019 when she traveled with her mother and stayed at the Barbara Fritchie AirBnB. During these three visits in Frederick, the artifacts of Barbara had been moved several times. While her church was going through renovations, the artifacts stored there were moved to the Frederick Historical Museum at 24 Church Street. During the same years, the replica of her home underwent changes of management and ownership a couple times moving the artifacts with much debate as to who owns them. A few of those items remain in the Barbara Fritchie House AirBnB, and some were kept by the woman who ran the house as the museum she managed, and some were sold into collectors' hands. So the pictures in these photos may be different from what one will be seeing on a visit to Frederick, Maryland. The newer church building holds a locked display case of many of Barbara's artifacts.

Barbara Fritchie

6

★ AN ABOLITIONIST ★

Barbara was an abolitionist which means she was very much against slavery. We know that the local community referred to her as being outspoken on her beliefs as an abolitionist, too. One example of this occurred after her husband, John died on November 10, 1849, and was buried in their church cemetery. She learned that the lawyer who was to represent his estate was a slave owner. She went to church and stood up addressing her congregation asking who would be willing to replace the current lawyer, and of course a member of her church said he would represent her husband's will and estate. He was a Christian and abolitionist so Barbara trusted his integrity and hired him. A historian from her church told the author that Barbara wanted to invest money that she inherited and would only go through a man who did not own slaves to make her investment. She was successful and made money from the investment. Rumor was that both Barbara and her husband had purchased slaves in the past to give them their freedom. There are only two known friends of hers who owned slaves. They were George Washington and Francis Scott Key.

As a young lady she discussed this concern with her friend George Washington on one of his many trips to Frederick, MD. He replied that his wife could not do without them. In his will, he said his 123 slaves would have their freedom upon his wife's death. Soon afterwards there was a fire at Martha's home and, fearing she may have been a target, she gave all the slaves their freedom immediately.

Later in life when Barbara was great friends with Francis Scott Key, she supposedly would also tell him to free his slaves. Francis was also concerned that his wife could not get along without the house slaves on whom she had grown dependent. Francis was born into a plantation family that owned slaves. He was originally against the abolitionist movement. How much of an influence Barbara had with his change of heart is unknown at this time, but he freed all his slaves and hired one of them to work as a foreman in the 1830's. He changed and started to represent slaves in court who were not granted their earned freedom from their slave owners. He was respected during this time by people who were black. However, when one slave was guilty of a serious crime, he helped to prosecute him like he would have done for any guilty person regardless of their race, but this gave Francis a bad reputation among people who were black. Some people accused him of being prejudiced even though he had changed his beliefs and was working hard to represent so many black people before this case.

A local Fredrick historian stated that Barbara was actually a slave owner and he thought that was hypocritical. This was shocking news! How could a woman so against slavery own a slave herself? Where was the proof? The historian had a record of slaves purchased one day showing a Barbara Ritchie on the record. Someone wrote over the original record and added an "F" in front of the name Ritchie. A look at the census records of Frederick showed many families with the last name Ritchie (who owned slaves) and also more than one household with a Barbara Fritchie. I noticed that Barbara's husband, John Fritchie, had a sister with a middle name of Barbara; her full name was Mary Barbara Fritchie. There are many examples of people of German heritage during that time period who were known by their middle name. John's sister, Barbara Fritchie, first married a Mr. Cary, and her second husband was Mr. Ritchie, probably making her the Barbara Ritchie in the slave records. The address of the slave owners is not given so how does one know for sure who the actual people were in these records? There is also a John Ritchie whose occupation is a lawyer in the Frederick census reports. Because his name was altered on the copy of the record sent to the author years ago to look like Fritchie, it is hard to know on which records one can rely for accuracy. The original records and copies made should never be written over the original writing or changed in any way. How does one know for sure which records actually belong to the Barbara Fritchie who waved the flag or her husband John Fritchie? Another Frederick historian who seemed very skilled in her occupation and was non-biased was asked and hired by the author to help research any and all slave records involving both Barbara and John. The author came across three more records on her own.

Those who believe Barbara could not have owned slaves are probably right

Barbara was well-known as an abolitionist and, as such, it is unlikely that she would have owned slaves. There is no mention by her neighbors, friends, church members, or family of her having any slaves in her home or in John's glove making business. They do, however, in several resources make note that she was an outspoken abolitionist who wanted an end to slavery. Whittier often wrote about Quakers and abolitionists. It is doubtful that he would have written such a poem to glorify someone who owned slaves. Because the copy of the original record given to the author from the slave auction was altered or changed to now show an "F" was added to the name of Ritchie, it does support a conspiracy theory rather than a document of truth. Historians and transcribers have a responsibility to leave documents as they are found and not tamper with them. The author would like to note that with the many Frederick local historians with who she communicated, she only found discrepancies with one of them that is mentioned throughout this book. No name is given to protect his identity, but important lessons can be learned from this experience. He is part of the reason for so much misinformation circulating so the opinions of that one historian and the author must be mentioned in this book. The author is so thankful for all the hard work and expertise of the many other historians from Frederick.

Those who believe Barbara could have owned slaves are probably right

If one believes that an abolitionist hates slavery, that person is also right. Looking at the time period in which they were living, they were faced with a minority of people who controlled politics, the laws, and much of what could be done to free or not free the slaves. Here is some important background information to understand first. In 1862, the total population in Maryland was 687,049. The total number of black people who were free was 83,942, and the total number of enslaved black people was 87,189. There were 110,278 households, of which 13,783 (or 12%) owned slaves. That means that for every one household with a slave there were nine who did not own any. So if more people did not believe in owning slaves then why did the majority let the minority make the decision to keep slaves? One answer is that some of the majority were small-time farmers or people of different occupations who did not have much say in the politics that took place. That was done by the big plantation owners who were wealthy and persuasive. They needed their slaves to keep their plantations going. Some abolitionists used what little money they had to start to buy slaves one at a time to give them their freedom. It was not effective because the wealthy just had more slaves brought in to replace them. The slave owners feared, however, that this practice of buying a slave to give them their freedom would hurt their business.

They made laws to prosecute anyone who continued to do that. There were new laws to govern the slave trade. After the new laws were in place, white people who tried to buy slaves and gave them their freedom could be tarred and feathered, hanged, or punished however the slave owners wanted. To earn freedom, a slave had to work 21 years for their master. Sometimes after the 21 years of service was completed, the master said they owed debt and had to work it off or found another way to delay the freedom papers.

Imagine someone receiving a slave as a gift from someone when they did not want to own a slave. They could be killed if they gave that person (slave) their freedom papers. One source says a plantation owner who did not like Barbara's sympathies toward the slaves decided to mock her. He brought her Henry Jones, a ten year old boy who he said was lame and of no use to him in the field. He gifted the slave to John which we know means John could not give Henry his freedom. John and Barbara took him in and taught him the trade of making gloves, and he worked in the shop alongside her husband for wages. When he was a young married adult, John and Barbara bought him a house of his own but had to keep it in their name legally. In John's will, he left the house to Henry after Barbara died, but, unfortunately, she had outlived Henry. The author went to the courthouse and obtained a copy of a John Fritchie's will (not knowing if this is the correct John Fritchie) which does state that Henry's house is given to him after Barbara's death.

There are slave auction records from Jan. 9, 1858 showing that a Barbara Fritchie bought an infant named George Davis as a gift for an Eliza Davis. Eliza was an older free black woman. George's mother Nancy Davis was a bi-racial slave, and, therefore, he was born into slavery. The purchase papers state that Barbara sold the baby to Eliza for the term of 20 years (the required years of service to earn freedom) with the understanding that he should be free at the age of twenty-one. Was this Eliza Davis the grandmother of George? Would Eliza be caring for her grandson George until his own mother was free and able to come for him? It is not known if this is "the" Barbara Fritchie or another woman with the same name such as John Fritchie's sister, Mary "Barbara" Fritchie who would have been known as Barbara Fritchie according to the German custom of going by the middle name as stated earlier. If it is the subject of this book, then Barbara found a clever way to keep this baby from real slavery.

Another situation involves a woman, Nancy Davis, who was a slave. Barbara bought her in order to arrange for her manumissions[11] papers for freedom. She was manumitted and set free by Bill of Sale on August 2, 1860 by a Barbara Fritchie. Nancy Davis lived in her own home as a free "mulato" as the census reports later shows. Although "mulato" is on the official records to describe a bi-racial person the author will use bi-racial instead in this book as the former word has become derogatory. These are the only cases involving a Barbara Fritchie; one involving a slave, Henry, that was gifted to her husband; one case when George was purchased to give as a gift to keep him in his family; and one case when Nancy was bought to give manumissions for freedom. Neither George nor Nancy ever appear in Barbara Fritchie's census report as living in her household. Citizens of Frederick, her follow church members, and family members have mentioned in many resources that Barbara never had slaves and that she was outspoken against slavery.

It is easy for those who live in modern times under different laws to look back in history and be judgmental. Some might say that it does not matter the reason why, owning a person, a human being, for any reason is wrong; period. But if Barbara felt that way, little George would have been sold to a different slave owner and raised working

---

[11] Manumissions is a historical term to release from slavery; set free.

the fields without ever knowing his parents or grandma. Historians and genealogists need to also investigate further when they find a record of someone purchasing a slave to see if they can find any census reports showing that the slaves were counted in their household. If not, they may have found the record of one of the abolitionists who bought a slave at auction only to help them obtain their freedom.

This map shows the division of the states during the American Civil War (1861-1865)

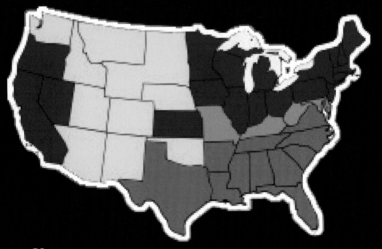

Key:

Blue for the U.S. Army's uniform color shows the 20 states that stayed in the Union.

Light blue represents the 5 border states that were part of the Union. Four of those states were permitted to keep slavery if they stayed in the Union and West Virginia was anti-slavery.

Grey represents the grey uniforms of the Confederacy and consisted of the 11 southern states that seceded.

The uncolored areas remained as territories.

7

★ A NATION DIVIDED ★

During the Civil War, the nation was divided between the states that chose to stay united in the Union and the Confederate states that chose to secede from the Union. The war even put neighbor against neighbor and family members against each other depending on which side they found their loyalties. Most of Barbara Fritchie's relatives were patriotic and supported the Union. One of Barbara's nephews on her husband's side was Valerious Ebert, a Southern sympathizer who supported the Confederates. He has said many misleading things about Barbara to try to discredit her story. Loyalty to one's cause often overpowered one's loyalty to family for many during this very divided time in history.

The Union was made up of the following northern states; Maine, New York, New Hampshire, Vermont, Massachusetts, Connecticut, Rhode Island, New Jersey, Pennsylvania, Ohio, Indiana, Illinois, Michigan, Wisconsin, Minnesota, Iowa, Kansas, Nevada, California, and Oregon. The Confederate states were Texas, Louisiana, Alabama, Arkansas, Tennessee, Georgia, South Carolina, North Carolina, Florida, Mississippi, and Virginia. And the Border States were Maryland, Missouri, Kentucky, Delaware, and West Virginia.

How Americans recorded the names of Civil War battles in their history books depicts what part of the United States they lived in or perhaps what part their Civil War ancestors were from. This time in history shows another division between the North and South as the Union named the battles fought after the nearest natural landmark, like a river or mountain and the Confederates named the battle after man-made features like towns, a railroad station, tavern, etc. Still today these battles are known by both names. Here are some of the examples:

Union Name	Civil War Battle Date/State	Confederate Name
Bull Run	July 21, 1861/Virginia	Manassas
Wilson's Creek	Aug. 10, 1861/Missouri	Oak Hills
Ball's Bluff	Oct. 21, 1861/Virginia	Leesburg
Battle of Logan's Cross Roads	Jan. 19, 1862/Kentucky	Battle of Mill Springs a.k.a Battle of Fishing Creek
Battle of Pea Ridge	March 7-8, 1862/Arkansas	Battle of Elkhorn Tavern
Pittsburg Landing	April 6-7, 1862/Tennessee	Shiloh
Fair Oaks	May 31 - June 1, 1862/Virginia	Seven Pines
Chickahominy	June 27, 1862/Virginia	The Battle of Cold Harbor a.k.a Gaines's Mill
2nd Battle of Bull Run	Aug. 28-30, 1862/Virginia	2nd Battle of Manassas
Chantilly	Sept. 1, 1862/Northern Virginia	Ox Hill
South Mountain	Sept. 14, 1862/Maryland	Boonsboro
Battle of Antietam	Sept. 17, 1862/Maryland	Battle of Sharpsburg
Chaplin Hills	Oct. 8, 1862/Kentucky	Perryville
Stone's River	Dec. 31, 1862 - Jan. 2, 1863/Tennessee	Murfreesboro
The Affair at Elk Creek	July 17, 1863/Oklahoma	The Engagement at Honey Springs
Olustee	Feb. 20, 1864/Florida	Ocean Pond
Sabine Cross Roads	Apr. 8, 1864/Louisiana	Mansfield
Opequon Creek	Sept. 19, 1864/Virginia	3rd Battle of Winchester

While it is true that during the war both sides named their battles, traditionally the one history records belongs to the victor. In this case, the Union names for the battles should be the ones in the American history books and the ones Americans refer to for the battle. The National Park Service has memorialized major battles of the War of Secession a.k.a. the War of the Rebellion that were fought in the South with signage showing the name the locals gave that battle, regardless

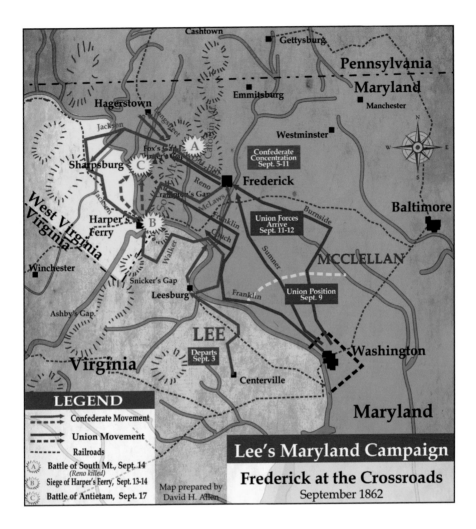

LEGEND

- ⇢ Confederate Movement
- ➡ Union Movement
- ---- Railroads
- A Battle of South Mt., Sept. 14 *(Reno killed)*
- B Siege of Harper's Ferry, Sept. 13-14
- C Battle of Antietam, Sept. 17

Map prepared by David H. Allen

Lee's Maryland Campaign

Frederick at the Crossroads

September 1862

of the victors. Some of these beautifully-preserved battle fields have biased signage only displaying the Southern name[12] rather than honoring the victors and displaying the Union name or, at the very least, labeling the area with both names for the historic accuracy of the battle.

---

[12] Examples: Manassas National Battlefield Park, Shiloh Battlefield, Shiloh National Military Park, Shiloh National Cemetery, Honey Springs Battlefield, and The 3rd Winchester Battlefield Park.

Dichotomizing the nation was not as clearly defined as making the Mason Dixon Line to distinguish the physical borders between the North and South, because the political and very emotional and spiritual divisions continued within states, between neighbors, and within households. Not only were the political views divided on whether or not to secede from the Union, but individuals found themselves divided on where their personal loyalties were.

The definition of what made a person with one black parent and one white parent a slave or not was also a strange division for mankind. Biologically, a child born to a white mother and black father was the same as a child born to a black mother and a white father, but legally it meant the difference between being born a free person or a slave. Though two children who were both 50% white and 50% black, under the former laws that divided these children into freeman or slaves, it was determined by the mother's status. That is incomprehensible in todays society. The following chart attempts to show how one's fate was determined.

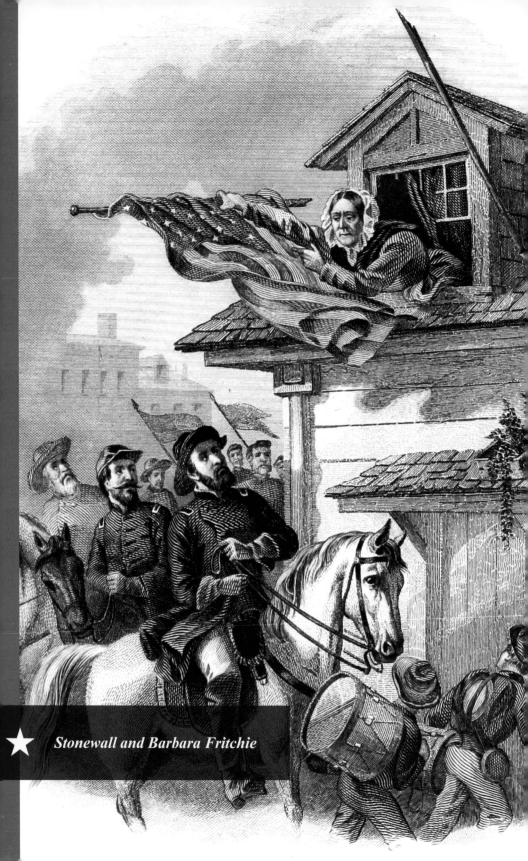

Stonewall and Barbara Fritchie

8

★ TAKING A LOOK AT STONEWALL JACKSON ★ FROM BOTH POINTS OF VIEW

By Guest Author Andrew Cooney

"Tyranny, like hell, is not easily conquered. But, we have this consolation in us that the harder the struggle the more glorious the triumph, tis dearness which gives everything its value"
-Thomas Paine

The determining factor of whether or not one is considered a patriot or a rebel, rests solely on the outcome of the conflict. History is written by the ones with the bloodiest swords, the victors. To arbitrarily determine one side as patriotic and another simply as rebellious or traitorous does a disservice to the moral, economic, and political struggles that serve as the cause of the conflict and a rallying cry to the men who chose to fight.

If the rebellious faction ends the conflict as the victor, the war is now viewed as a war of independence with their soldiers being patriots for the cause. When the rebellious faction loses the conflict and is brought back into the fold of the political system they fought against, they are henceforth viewed as rebellious traitors. It is a very fine line between the two and highlights the need for an empirical perspective.

It used to be that a civil war was defined as being a conflict between two factions of the same nation, fighting for control of the political system. In the American Civil War, this wasn't the case, as the Confederate states were fighting for emancipation from the United States. It wasn't control of the existing system, but the creation of a new one which led them toward secession.

General Thomas "Stonewall" Jackson is one of the most famous participants of the American Civil War. Even today, he is still largely seen as a military hero and one of the most formidable generals fielded by either side during the war. Some historians have even gone so far as to reasonably speculate the war could have had a different outcome had he not been killed by friendly fire during the Battle of Chancellorsville in May of 1863.

It is important to remember, that pre-civil war United States was a very different place than it is today. The federal government was much more decentralized and states held a strong level of autonomy. People were loyal to their home state first and foremost, and most of the actual political governance was done on a state level. Even the military during the war was organized by the states from which the troops originated.

It is easy to question why someone had the loyalties they did or made the choices they made when reflecting back equipped with the ultimate power of hindsight. With Stonewall, the choices and decisions he made are all relatively clear on display for us to see. He was a devout Christian; he loved his wife, his nation, and his home state of Virginia.

General Jackson attended the U.S Military Academy at West Point where, upon graduation in 1846, he accepted a commission as an artillery officer and served in the Mexican War. During the Mexican

War, he excelled at tactics, and his bravery under fire became well-known throughout the ranks. In a short two years, he left the war as a brevet major, opting to stay in the military until taking a teaching position at the Virginia Military Institute. The same VMI is famous for their cadets forming their own regiment in the defense of New Market.

Jackson was met with mixed response from most of the cadets at VMI, as most professors are by their students. Although, he certainly could not have planned for it, his time as a professor was invaluable as it refined his own understanding of tactics which only served to compliment his prior battlefield experience.

Following Virginia's secession from the Union in 1861, Stonewall accepted a commission as a Colonel in the Virginia militia at Harpers Ferry. After being promoted to Brigadier General, Jackson directly led "Virginia's First Brigade" at the Battle of First Manassas, or First Bull Run as the Union named it. First Manassas was the first major battle of the war and both armies were fielding raw recruits who had a tendency to panic and shun discipline as the gore and horror of steel and shot took its toll.

The Confederate lines were breaking, and it looked as if the day was going to be lost with their left flank faltering. General Jackson, being the experienced strategist, placed his brigade on just under the crest of Henry House Hill, so that the Union Troops pursuing the fleeing Confederate, would only see them after fully exposing themselves on top of the hill.

General Bernard Bee is credited during this moment to have called out to his men who were still fleeing, " Look! There is Jackson standing like a stone wall. Rally behind the Virginians!"

The retreating Confederate troops, seeing the almost surreal image of the Virginians holding the line like coastal rock holding back the sea, turned about and reformed with the newly dubbed "Stonewall Brigade". The counter-push that followed created havoc and panic among the Union troops, resulting in a Confederate Victory.

It is said that, when asked how General Jackson could be so calm and collected under fire, he replied along the lines of "God knows when my time is up and I cannot change or argue with that."

General Jackson also became well-known for his forced marches, where his men could cover more ground in a single day than any other, giving them increased tactical maneuverability. He could ask more of his men than other generals could, while still having them deliver. It is speculation, but I believe this to be because of the actions they all witnessed during what was, for many of them, their first brush with combat. The fact he knew so many victories due to his strategies could only have served to bolster this unwavering faith in him that many of his men had.

By today's standards, one could argue that General Jackson was a traitor to the United States, as we know it, for choosing to fight with his state rather than his country. However, I think the type of man General Jackson was and the actions and decisions he consistently made refutes any notion of him being a self-aggrandising figure.

I firmly believe he fought for the side of his conscience and for what he valued in autonomous and free statehood. Whether that makes him a traitor, rebel, patriot or something else, truly doesn't matter because he fought for and stood beside his principles and served as a beacon of hope amongst a backdrop of monumental dismay for so many in such desperate times. It is perhaps best to remember men for who they were, rather than how they would fit into society today.

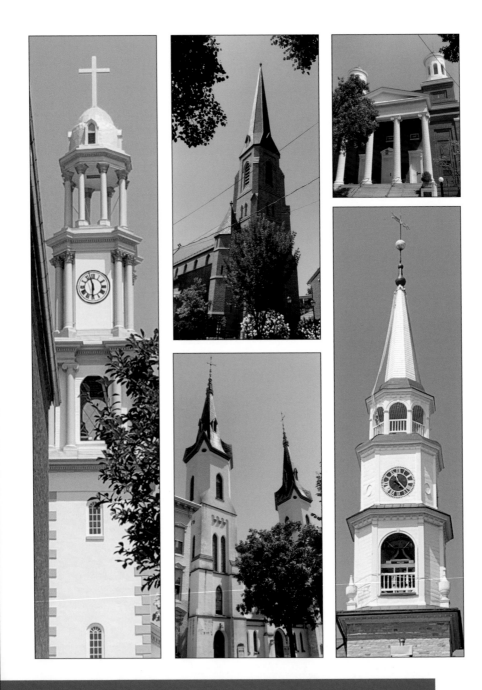

These pictures of the "Spires of Frederick Town" referred to in Whittier's poem were taken by the author in August, 2019.

9

★ WHITTIER INSPIRES THE UNION ★

John Greenleaf Whittier (1807 – 1892) was born in Massachusetts and was a self-educated Quaker who was a crusader and active in the fight against slavery. He published his first book, Legends of New England in Prose and Verse, in 1831. All of his work was about nature, non-fiction, real-life events, or real people. Some of his early work was about nature and his love for his country. He published pamphlets and lectured against slavery. Whittier was a member of the legislature of Massachusetts serving from 1834 – 1835. In 1842, he ran for the U.S. Congress on the Liberty ticket. In 1854 he was a founding member of the Republican Party. During this political involvement, he still managed to steadily publish his work.

Inspirational songs and poems were often written by people to motivate the troops in times of war. The Civil War called for an inspirational poem to rally the Union, and Whittier answered that call when he penned the Barbara Freitchie poem. He wrote the poem based on the facts that were given to him by several reliable sources and from the papers of the time describing Barbara's brave actions. He used the German spelling of her name as it would have originally been spelled by her husband's German ancestors. As one approaches Frederick, there is a majestic cluster of spires quite visible from the many churches close together along the appropriately named Church Street. Unfortunately, his poem does not state which day in September the incident occurred. The Maryland Campaign took place over several different nearby battles in September taking Jackson through Frederick or camping just outside the city on several occasions. Because we know that General Jesse Lee Reno had visited with Barbara about her flag waving incident we know it took place prior to his death in the Battle of South Mountain on September 14, 1862. The Border State during war would have had its citizens displaying both the Confederate flags and the Union flags depending on which political views one shared. There are accounts of the Confederates marching through town and a couple of women who supported them going out into the street and pinning a little Confederate flag on the hat of one person and on the jacket of another. They waved their Confederate flags and cheered as the Confederates marched through. A week later, the opposite was happening where the Union flags were waving and people were cheering the troops. It seems no different than today when we have a political campaign, and the yards are filled with signs for the different political parties. When Whittier used the number 40 in his poem, it did more than emphasize that both Union and Confederate flags were waved in equal numbers in Frederick, it was a number used in the Bible to show a time of trial was among them.[13] The author is assuming that Whittier's point was to refer to this Civil War as a time of trial. For the citizens of Frederick, it was also a time of trial when there was such divide among their loyalties.

---

[13] In the Old Testament, God told Noah that it would rain for 40 days and 40 nights (Genesis 7:12). Moses killed an Egyptian and escaped to Midian where he spent 40 years in the desert (Acts 7:30). Moses was on Mount Sinai for 40 days and 40 nights in (Exodus 24:18). The Israelites wandered for 40 years (Deuteronomy 8:2-5). Israel served the Philistines for 40 years (Judges 13:1). Goliath was unbeatable against Saul's army for 40 days before David arrived to defeat him with just his slingshot (1 Samuel 17:16). In the New Testament, Jesus was tempted for 40 days and 40 nights (Mathew 4:2). After Jesus' Resurrection there were 40 days before the Ascension (Acts 1:3). The number 40 is also used in the following; Deuteronomy 9:18, 25; Deuteronomy 25:3; Numbers 13:25; 1 Kings 19:8; Ezekiel 4:6; 29:11-13; Jonah 3:4 no doubt it is found in the Bible more times.

When the author was on a Civil War tour of Frederick, she was told that some historians still believe that, if the Union had not arrested some voting delegates with Confederate loyalties right before the vote for secession, the vote would have passed.

Stonewall Jackson's widow thanked Whittier for showing the more compassionate side of Jackson in the poem. She believed the poem was an accurate account of what happened. In her later years of life she tried to debunk the story.

Whittier explained that he did not create or embellish Barbara's story but had read it in reports from several newspapers of the time and considered it from trustworthy sources.

Mr. Whittier, writing March 7, 1862, informs further that he "also received letters from several other responsible persons wholly or partially confirming the story, among whom was the late Dorothea L. Dix".[14]

Dorothea Dix (1805 - 1887) served as Superintendent of Women Nurses during the Civil War. Barbara Fritchie was one of many women who volunteered to help her in the many hospitals set up in Frederick, MD, during the Civil War.

Office of Women Nurses,
U. S. Hospital Service, Washington D.C.
January 12th 1865.

To J.G. Whittier, Esq'

Sir; Lately being in Frederick City on Hospital Inspection, I learned some facts concerning "Barbara Frietchie," whose name is almost immortalized in our patriotic poem.

---

[14] Source: *Battles and Leaders of the Civil War.* civilwarhome.com.

"Up from the meadows rich with corn"; And I obtained from a member of her family the carte which I enclose, believing if you do not already possess it, you will be gratified to receive what is said by her friends to be a very excellent likeness.

Barbara Frietchie had not become disabled from performing many duties and pleasant offices of life, though of so advanced years. Till a few weeks before her decease, she prepared delicacies for sick soldiers in the Hospitals. Knitting was a favorite emolument. Her house was a model of order, and neat habits had always characterized her domestic life. She was remarkably fond of her garden and was singularly successful in the cultivation of flowers, of which she had the earliest and finest varieties. Indeed whenever, on festive occasions, choice flowers were in request, "Aunt Barbara's" liberal hand bestowed the most beautiful and fragrant.

She was fond of children - but she expected they should regard her orders. I fear (not any) who were unruly, or who failed to regard her cleanly scoured floors, could expect the nice cakes and apples she held in store to dispense to all "good boys and girls." She received her relatives and friends on her last birthday, presenting in the old fashion nuts, cakes and wine.

To the last, she testified in inspiring terms her abhorrence of Treason and Traitors; she walked "resting upon a staff," and carried an air of dignified venerable age, always respected. She is remembered with affection, and those who had known her intimately for half a century and more, were her most devoted friends.

I have nothing to add more of this remarkable woman, but in conclusion, I desire to express to you my sentiments of respect, and to acknowledge myself long your debtor in the instruction and enjoyment derived from your poetical books.

D. L. Dix
Superintendent
U.S. Hospital Nurses

Note in the letter from Dorothea Dix, she mentions that she enclosed a picture of Barbara which is another example of there being more than one picture taken of Barbara. Also, it mentions that Barbara had additional income from her knitting.

Writing to the editor of "The Century" on the 10th of June, 1886, Mr. Whittier said: "The poem 'Barbara Frietchie' was written in good faith. The story was no invention of mine. It came to me from sources which I regarded as entirely reliable: it had been published in newspapers, and had gained public credence in Washington and Maryland before my poem was written. I had no reason to doubt its accuracy then, and I am still constrained to believe that it had foundation in fact. If I thought otherwise, I should not hesitate to express it. I have no pride of authorship to interfere with thy allegiance to truth."

To one of many friends who asked Whittier if Barbara was a myth, Whittier answered in a letter dated October 19, 1890: "I had a portrait of the good lady Barbara from the saintly hand of Dorothea Dix, whose life is spent in works of love and duty..." and he confirmed that his poem was factual.

He was questioned many times by people asking if it were a true story or not and to reveal who his sources were. He always said in his many responses that he had **many reliable sources** and that it was true. He never named Mrs. E.D.E.N. Southworth[15] as a source whom historians falsely list as his only source for the poem, but she could have well been one of his many sources. Whittier also did not believe Mary Quantrill's story and never bothered to reply to Mary who wrote to him once several years later saying she was the true Barbara and wanted him to acknowledge that.

---

[15] Emma Dorothy Eliza Nevitte Southworth (December 26, 1819 – June 30, 1899) was an American writer of more than 60 novels in the latter part of the 19th century. Her popular books were *The Hidden Hand and Ishmael.*

Maude Allana (Cooper) Thayer with her dog Fritz named after Barbara Fritchie because both displayed the same feistiness.

10

★ THE ALLEGED COVER-UP BEGINS ★

When Stonewall was touched by Barbara's patriotic stance, he showed compassion for an elderly woman and was simply showing the human side of himself and not the soldier in those moments. However, that is the opinion of this author, but for some of his men, they were very worried that this would be taken as a 'sign of weakness' for their General if the word got out that their General spared an old woman. That night at their camp, a few of his men asked him what they should do. Stonewall did not seem to be bothered by the whole thing and did not think it was important. He never made any public statements to either admit or deny the incident occurred. He must have mentioned it to his wife, however, as many years later she told Whittier that she was thankful to him for portraying her husband as compassionate towards Barbara. Several of his men decided they needed to try to debunk the whole story to protect their General's reputation. These men sat under a tree at the camp and plotted out how to change this story around. This story was discovered many years later when one of their diaries was found by his own family after he died. Another of these men, Henry Kyd Douglas, was a big part of the cover-up and told people he was with Stonewall the whole time while in Frederick and that the flag waving never happened.

The cover-up would have been more believable if they just denied it happened and left it at that. The more they tried to get people who were Southern sympathizers to back up their story, the more their lies became so exaggerated that it becomes unbelievable. They also didn't collaborate on their cover-up stories so none of them match or support what the other had already said. For example, it is well known that Barbara was in great health and very active at her old age. Jacob Engelbrecht states that in his diary. Dorothy Dix states that Barbara was volunteering to help with the wounded in the hospitals. She states Barbara wasn't sick until the last week of her life. Yet Barbara's nephew from her husband's side, Valerius Ebert, states that she was blind, lost most of her mobility, and was bed-ridden. He was a known Confederate, and that alone was his motive to put his southern loyalty above family. Her church has a printed timeline of events, and it states that when she celebrated her birthday, she came down with a bad cold that turned to pneumonia just 15 days before she died. After the Confederate occupation was long gone and the Union came through town, General Jesse Reno visited Barbara wanting to hear the story of her flag waving first-hand from Barbara herself. He said she was very hospitable and served him her homemade wine as she told him the story of the flag incident with Jackson. He asked to use her writing desk to write home. She served him some of her homemade food to his delight. He asked for the flag she used to wave at Jackson and his men. She did not want to part with that one and gave him another flag. Unfortunately, it is in the next battle that Jesse was killed, and they found under his body the flag from Barbara that he treasured. That flag was given to his family at first, who later donated it to the museum to display 'the flag that Reno was gifted from Barbara'.

Douglas who served under Jackson and was a part of the cover-up, originally had many people around Frederick believing him. He wrote a book, I Rode with Stonewall. He did some public speaking about it as well. There are many inconsistencies discussed later about his cover-up. He kept changing his story about what Jackson did during his time in Frederick. The letter he came up with supposedly from Jackson to Rev. Ross and his story about Jackson needing an ambulance wasn't in his original manuscript at all and was added in time for his revision of the story.

The Confederate Veteran is a publication written for the southern sympathizers. They published a sarcastic spoof of the Barbara Freitchie poem in 1893. Their article is called, "Barbara Frietchie Revised." In this mockery, they say she was bed-ridden, blind, and deaf among many other things. The reader should know in the very manner it was written and from the source that published it not to take it seriously or for its word. However, after it was printed, many of the comments about Barbara were quoted as fact in other letters to the editor in other newspapers.

Confederate Veteran
By Confederated Southern Memorial Association
(U.S.) Sons of Confederate Veterans (Organization);
United Confederate Veterans;
United Daughters of the Confederacy.

The cover-up becomes so obvious if one looks at all the letters to the editor and the articles written about Barbara and divide them into two piles; one pile supporting Barbara and her flag waving, and the second pile trying to denounce her story. Now look again at each pile and look at the sources for each. It became so clear to this author that all the people who knew Barbara and supported her story were also supporting the Union with three exceptions. One of those exceptions was the very soldier who fired at her and he signed his letter to the editor from an ex-confederate. Most of the sources who try to debunk her story are Confederates or people who have quoted them and believed their story. You be the judge after reading the following articles and learning their biases. The newspaper articles in support of Barbara are printed in blue ink and the articles against her story are printed in grey ink.

Published Monday, February 15, 1869, page 2:

BARBARA FRITCHIE.
Who Waved the Flag at Fredericksburg?

To the Editor of the Washington Star

The attack upon my son in an article from a New-York paper copied in the Star, demanded his defense, and in making it, to support the loyalty of his family, he alluded to my vindication of the National flag in the City of Frederick, Md., Sept. 6, 1862. In your issue of the 5th inst. you remark in reference to his allusion to me, "if Mr. Quantrill can establish this fact he should do so at once," &c. Passing by the hotel tone of society in that city during the war, which doubtless affected my interests proportionably as much as those of any other, I shall submit to the public an extract from a private letter written by me on the 12th let., which may afford some amusement, and at the same time prove how easy a matter it is for even journalists, in these sensational times, to be imposed upon:

By the setting of the sun on the eve of the date already given, a stranger might have paused in the streets of Frederick, and asked, what "change has come over the sport" of this city? Not a flag was to be seen; not a citizen upon its streets; the pulse of business (never very strong) had almost ceased to beat; and as friend met friend, they whispered with white lips of the approach fo the enemy. It was true. Gen. ROBERT LEE, at the head of the Confederate army, was marching on Frederick, left in the main with its women and children, (I speak of loyal portion) to the mercy of a chivalrous enemy. Gen. Stonewall JACKSON entered the city on Saturday, the 6th of September, and Gen. LONGSTREET on the following Monday came in with the remaining forces. So far as I am informed, as good order prevailed as could be expected under the circumstances.

Their sojourn was brief, for the morning of the 10th raised the curtain, and the scene presented was truly warlike. Day dawned upon marching columns of infantry, calvary and artillery, wending their way to South Mountain and Antitem. Onward they pressed, presenting little variety, excepting national flags were tied to horses' tails, and trailed through the streets, as a warning to Unionists of what might occur thereafter. Seated at my door, I had been a silent observer of the morning's pageant. It may be well to state here, although I had not the acquaintance of a solitary Confederate soldier, save those who had been my neighbors, the house where the United States flag floated under more friendly auspices, was known to many. To continue: Music was swelling, the stars and bars were waving, and as I gazed upon brave men enduring every degree of danger and sugaring for what they called their rights, my reverie was interrupted by the sudden halt of a subordinate officer before my door, who shouted at the top of his voice, "G-d d—m the stars and stripes to the dust, with all who advocate them!" The hero was borne off by the dense throng, but the insult admitted of no second thought. The flag of my country, sacred to the memory of my grandsires, and to the best men of Revolutionary history, damned to the dust! It was too much! My little daughter, who had been enjoying her flageolet secretly, at this moment came to the door, attracted by this blasphemous salute, and, taking it from her hand, I held it firmly in my own, but not a word was spoken. Soon a bright spot in this motley mass was visible. A splendid carriage, accompanied by elegantly mounted officers, evidently the flower of the army, was approaching. As they came near the house they caught the glimpse of the tiny flag, and exclaimed, "See! See! The flag, the Stars and Stripes!" And, with true chivalry, hats were removed and courtesies were offered the bearer, but not her standard. They had advanced some paces when a halt was ordered, and soon a lady-then Miss MARTHA SINN, since Mrs. JAMES ARNOLD-of Frederick, standing near with other ladies of the neighborhood, admonished me to fly with my colors. I did not fly, however, nor move, until an officer from the above-named company rode up, and directing his attention to me, I stepped forward, and the following remarks were exchanged:

Officer-Madam, give me your flag.

Answer-No, Sir, you can't have it.

Officer-Give me your flag to present to Gen. Lee.

Answer-Gen. Lee cannot have my flag.

Officer-Why?

Answer-I think it worthy of a better cause.

Officer-Your flag has been dishonored.

Answer-Only by the cause you have espoused.

Officer, (regarding me sternly.)-Come down South, and we will show you whole negro brigades equipped for the service of the United States.

Answer-I am informed on that subject.

Here a brother officer warned him of the value of time, and urged a return, which was accordingly made. The Confederate soldier said the officer who asked the flag was Gen. Hill.

I remained in the same position, resting the staff of my flaglet on the railing of the porch, musing upon the incident which had just transpired, when a soldier, who, it appeared, had heard the remarks, stepped behind me, and with his bayonet cut off my staff close to my hand. The report resembled that of a pistol, and turning about I saw him tear my flag into pieces, and stamp them in the dust. I pronounced this the act of a coward, and again turned to view the army. Among the young ladies present, but who died about the close of the war, was Miss MARY HOPWOOD, daughter of Mr. JAMES HOPWOOD, well known as a Union citizen of Frederick. Seeing my flag cut down, she drew a concealed flageolet from her sleeve and supplied the place of mine. In another instant the second flag was cut down by the same man. As soon as the information was conveyed to the officers, one man, more advanced in years than either of those already referred to, came back to the spot and reproved in sharp language the man who cut down my flags.

In conclusion, I can endorse every word of S. G. MERRILL'S statement. Mrs. BARBARA FRITCHIE was held in high esteem by the people of Frederick City, and the ladies generally are second to none for their devotion to the cause of our country.

MARY A. QUANTRILL.
Washington City, D.C., Feb. 9, 1869.

Mary confirms in this statement that it was Jackson entering town on September 6, (which is the date when Barbara was the first to wave the flag to Jackson), and Mary states that her incident occurred on the 10th when she waved it to possibly Gen. Hill. This confirms that the two incidents happened on different days. Whittier wrote the poem about Jackson, not Hill. Therefore, the poem is not written about Mary.

Published February 25, 1869 in the New York Times, page 2

Barbara Fritchie Once More—Letter from Mr. Whittier.
From the Washington Star, Feb. 23

Recently a communication appeared in the Star claiming for Mrs. M.A. QUANTRILL that she is entitled to the honors given to BARBARA FRITCHIE, (immortalized in WHITTIER'S stirring verse,) for displaying the Stars and Stripes while the rebel troops were passing through Frederick. We have now from Mr. Whittier the following letter, in which he holds to his faith in BARBARA, and gives good reason for so doing. As there is no doubt, from the testimony of at least four witnesses, that Mrs. QUANTRILL'S claim is well-founded, there seems to be considerable mystification in the matter. Probably the true solution is that both these brave Union women displayed their patriotism and their courage in the same way on the same occasion:

To the Editor of the Star:

I have received a copy of thy paper, containing a letter from a lady who claims to have been the heroine of the flag at Frederick. I have never heard of her before, and of course know nothing of her veracity or loyalty. I must say, however, in justice to myself, that I have full confidence in the truth of the original statement furnished me by a distinguished literary lady of Washington, as respects BARBARA FRITCHIE—a statement soon after confirmed by DOROTHEA DIX, who visited Frederick, and made herself acquainted with many interesting particulars of the life and character of that remarkable woman.

Very truly, thy friend,
JOHN G. WHITTIER.
Amesbury, 19th 2nd mo., 1869

In this letter to the editor please note the whole first half is not written by Whittier but it is a prelude written by the newspaper editor with his "opinions" of Whittier's intentions. This editor's statement that, "… As there is no doubt, from the testimony of a least four witnesses, that Mrs. Quantrill's claim is well-founded, there seems to be considerable mystification in the matter. Probably the true solution is that both these brave Union women displayed their patriotism…". This editor has now misled the reader to believe these are Whittier's thoughts as well, which they are clearly not. Whittier states he never heard of Mary Quantrill before now. On a side note, this also confirms that theory made by a couple people that, in his poem, his use of the plural word "stars" was referring to a blending of Mary's and Barbara's incidents and that he combined them. This author believes all the famous "stars" to have lived in Frederick prior to his writing of the poem like Francis Scott Key and Barbara may have been his reason for the plural use. Because the newspaper editor injected his own opinion before Whittier's own words, it led to future misquoted statements saying that it was Whittier who said he may have gotten the two stories mixed up, when he says just the opposite.

Published Saturday, April 17, 1869 in the New York Times on page 4:

Barbara Fritchie Again.

A correspondent of the Washington Star says:

"I premise by saying that I am a native of Frederick City, and have known the FRITCHIE family all my lifetime, and that it is one of the most respectable of the entire community; and it has been a surprise to me that no one has ventured upon a vindication of her claims to honor which the poet has given her. BARBARA FRITCHIE was a reality at the time referred to. When JACKSON was passing through Frederick, of necessity he had to pass the house in which she lived, on West Patrick street, south side, next to Carrol Creek. As he and his troops passed her house, she appeared at the dormer window of her one-storied house and waved the Stars and Stripes before their veritable faces. One of his men raised his gun toward her, and she cried 'Shoot! Shoot!' Still waving her flag. JACKSON himself knocked his gun aside, and commanded him not to attempt any such thing, at the same time raising his hat in honor of the flag. A shout then went up from his own men, and they passed on. This is the gist of the story which I have often heard in Frederick, and never heard it contradicted by anyone. Mrs. QUANTRILL'S story may be true, but I never heard it before I saw it in your paper."

Published in the New York Times April 15, 1875 on page 9:

Barbara Fritchie Again.

The following appears as a communication in the San Francisco Bulletin:
Editor Bulletin: I saw in your paper of the 26th an item concerning Barbara Fritchie. It denied the fact that she held the flag in her window during the march through Frederick. She did, for I was in one of the dust-browned ranks (may I be pardoned) that Stonewall ordered to halt, and I flatter myself that the bullet from my gun was one of the many that hit the flag.

An Ex-Confederate.
Los Angeles, April 2, 1875

Published in the New York Times April 26, 1875 page 8:

BARBARA FRITCHIE.
THE PLEASANT STORY CONCERNING HER EXPLODED.
ADDITIONAL TESTIMONY SHOWING THAT
SHE NEVER WAVED THE FLAG IN THE FACE
OF STONEWALL JACKSON'S TROOPS
—WHITTIER'S POEM.
From the Baltimore Sun, April 24.

There was published some days ago a card found in a California paper, dated at Los Angeles, and signed "An ex-Confederate," which revived the fiction of Barbara Fritchie, of Frederick, Md., on which was founded Whittier's poem recounting the pretended incident of the troops under Stonewall Jackson firing upon, by his order, and striking down the national flag suspended over the dame's house when they entered Frederick in 1962, and which the dame heroically seized and held aloft herself afterward. Long ago it was pretty well established in all this section of country that the story had no proper foundation, and that, therefore, the imagination of the famous New-England poet had soared away on even a less substantial Pegasus than usual. But the hardihood of the "ex-Confederate." As he styled himself, who asseverated at this late day the truth of the story. And stated that he was one of Jackson's men who, at his order, fired upon Barbara Fritchie's flag, excited curiosity as to what its publication might elicit. We have already published from our correspondent at Frederick a brief statement showing how incorrect the Fritchie story is, and we have now fuller communications from other sources which completely dissipate the whole matter. We subjoin the poem, and wish its lofty numbers had been fitted to a more worthy and truthful theme:

(The author chose not to reprint the poem that you already know here.)

These are good verses, but the iconoclastic hand of fact rudely demolishes them in every respect save that of their polished meter and ringing sonorousness. Miss Esmeralda Boyle, daughter of the late Commodore Boyle, United States Navy, who was a Baltimorean, is engaged in the preparation of a Maryland biographical history, and Whittier's Barbara Fritchie, of course, engaged her attention. Unlike Whittier, she doubted the story, inquired and analyzed, and obtained the following indisputable evidence of its utter falsity. The writer of the first letter, Jacob Engelbrecht, is an excellent old citizen of Frederick, greatly respected for his integrity, once Mayor of the city, and notably an oracle in the matter of dates and occurrences, he having, for many years, kept a diary of events. The other letter is from Samuel Tyler, Esq., a native of Frederick, well known for his skill in historic lore and varied literary accomplishments, and as the author of the life of Chief Justice Taney. The evidence is entirely conclusive in the premises, and relegates Barbara Fritchie to the humble obscurity she had attained before Whittier made her famous with more poetry than truth.

JACOB ENGELBRECHT'S STATEMENT.
FREDERICK, MD., JUNE 30, 1874.

My Dear Sir: In answer to yours of the 27th instant, I would say that I have known Mrs. Barbara Fritchie nearly all my life, and lived directly opposite to her for thirty-six years, (from 1826 to 1862). Mrs. Fritchie was always a nice old lady, who "along the cool sequestered vale of life kept the noiseless tenor of her way." Several years before her death she requested me to transcribe from their old family German Bible the family records into another Bible, now in the hands of her niece, Mrs. Hanshaw.

Mrs. Barbara Fritchie was born in Lancaster, Penn., Dec. 3, 1766, and died in Frederick Dec 18, 1862, aged ninety-six years and fifteen days. Her husband, Mr. John C. Fritchie, died November 10, 1846. Mrs. Fritchie's maiden name was 'Hauer.' Mrs. Fritchie never had any children. With respect to the flag-waving, I know nothing about it; neither did I ever hear of any person in our city who knew anything about it. The first that I heard of it was in Harper's Monthly.

When Gen. Lee passed through our city with his army I was very anxious to see all I could. I therefore posted myself at one of the upstairs windows, where I had a full view of all that passed below in the street. When Gen. Lee got in front of Mrs. Fritchie's house, and also in front of mine, he and his whole army halted, and I afterward ascertained (this, you know, was in West Patrick street) that Gen. Stonewall Jackson, (who had been encamped north of our city,) with his army, was coming up Mill alley or Bentz street. So Gen. Lee waited until Gen. Jackson and his army had passed. All the time that Gen. Lee stopped in front of Mrs. Fritchies house I saw no flag waving. If there had been I certainly would have seen it, and as for Gen. Jackson, he did not pass over the bridge, but passed up another street.

When Gen. Lee's army had possession of Frederick we Union people were very cautious with our flags—had them all secreted. It being the first time our city was captured, we rather all felt unpleasant. Afterward, when we were captured by Gen. Jubal Early, (the $200,000 man,) we were not quite so much frightened.

If there was anything like flag-waving at Mrs. Fritchie's house, I think it was when Gen. McClellan's army passed through in pursuit of Gen. Lee, four or five days after. When McClellan's army passed through our city we were all jubilant, and, of course, came out with our flags to show we were Union. One of my family is under the impression that Mrs. Fritchie came out with her small flag to the front door, and at the same time an officer was passing who supposed that form her manner of holding it had intended it for him: he accordingly reached up and she handed it to him. This, I think, is all about the flag-waving. The fact is, Mrs. Fritchie had no flag in the house of a larger size than twelve or sixteen inches square. The most courageous part that I noticed of her conduct during our capture was that in her coming home from her niece's one day the front of her house was full of rebel soldiers, (who were sitting in the shade,) when she pushed her cane between them (the steps were all full) and said: "Get up, you dirty fellows, and let me in."

I have now tried to give you all the information that I can on this Whittier poem business. If anything of the kind had taken place I think I should have known or heard of it. I was a the front window up stairs nearly the whole time the invading troops were passing; hardly ate my meals, except when one corps had passed; there was a stoppage of sometimes an hour or two-forever, I was anxious to know what length of time it would take them to pass. Such things I wanted to know to put in my diary. (By the by, I have been keeping a regular diary for fifty-four years—since 1820.). I was not Mayor of Frederick at the time Gen. Lee went through our city. I was Mayor from March, 1865, to 1868.

I am now an old man, seventy-six and a half years old, born Dec. 11, 1797, past three-score years and fifteen. Of our family (old family) out of the six brothers only two remain. Michael, at the age of eighty-two, is tolerably well; of course, we all feel old. With friendly respects.

JACOB ENGLEBRECHT.

Prof. SAMUEL TYLER, Georgetown, D.C.:

PROF. SAMUEL TYLER'S STATEMENT.

MY DEAR MISS BOYLE: In answer to your inquiry about the origin of the poem, "Barbara Fritchie," by Whittier, I can say that it was repeated to me soon after it was written by some one, who informed me who the person was that had communicated the facts of the poem to Whittier. I remarked that it was strange how such facts came to be connected with so obscure a person as Barbara Fritchie, who I supposed must be the wife of John Fritchie, the glover, who lived on Patrick street, Frederick, Md., near the bridge over Carroll Creek, where it intersects that street. The answer was that she was a person. I remarked that Stonewall Jackson had never passed Barbara Fritchie's house, but passed down Mill alley, from the north of Frederick, and entered Patrick street on the west side of Carroll Creek, while Barbara Fritchie's house is on the east side. He was marching for Harper's Ferry, and Barbara Fritchie's house was out of the his way from his encampment. He and his staff passed down Second street, north of Patrick street, and he dismounted from his horse at the door of Rev. John B. Ross's house, and wrote on a card the following note, and slid it under the door, and rode off to Mill alley, and down it to Patrick street:

Regret not being permitted to see Dr. and Mrs. Ross: but could not expect to have that pleasure at so unreasonable an hour.

T.J. Jackson

Sept. 10, 1862—5:15 A.M.

Such, with its abrupt beginning, is the whole note, indicating great haste.

Mr. Ross' house was diagonally opposite my house. I read the note not long after it was written, and have procured a copy of it from Mrs. Ross. Mrs Ross is a daughter of the late Gov. McDowell, of Virginia, and was an intimate friend of Gen. Jackson's, at Lexington, Va., hence his note.

While Gen. Reno, who was killed at South Mountain, was passing Barbara Fritchie's house with the United States troops, as I have heard, a little girl held at the window a small United States flag. Barbara Fritchie was at the window, then about ninety-six years old, and it is likely out of these facts the imaginative informant gave Whittier the ideas of the poem. All that relates to the Confederate General and his troops is pure fiction. Yours truly,

SAMUEL TYLER

GEORGETOWN, D.C., Feb. 20, 1875.

To Miss Esmerelda Boyle.

The note from Jackson to Dr. Ross has been disproved and it is thought that it was created by Douglas as part of the cover-up. Englebrecht, as stated earlier could not have seen Barbara from her side window facing her creek. Samuel Tyler had Confederate loyalties as a former member of Jackson's staff that would lead him to join the cover-up against Barbara. He wrote a book about Judge Taney who sided with the secession although he didn't resign from the Supreme Court.

Published in the New York Times on May 16, 1869 on page 3:

The Demolition of the Home of Barbara Fritchie.
From the Frederick (Md.) Examiner.

The last remnant of the old house where BARBARA FRITCHIE lived and toiled has been removed, and laborers are now employed in engaging some ten feet below the original foundation, as if to root out the spot of earth upon which it stood. A few days more and the tourist, the patriot, and the poet will have pointed to them the muddy waters of Carroll Creek where once stood the weird old home of faithful defender of her country's flag.

It seems to have been the determination of our city authorities to erase from the memory of man that the "Fritchie woman" ever lived, and guided by this desire the first step was to destroy the house in which she had lived, and where Stonewall Jackson

"Shoot if you must, this old gray head,
But spare your country's flag, she said,"

and to the accomplishment of this object they turned all the genius and ability with which nature has so liberally gifted them. They first passed an ordinance to widen and straighten Caroll Creek. They then decided that the Fritchie house was in the line of the proposed improvements, and then agreed to "wipe the damned thing out."

"Barbara Fritchie's work is o'er,
The rebel rides his raids no more."

Yet the spirit was predominant, and to gratify the hatred of the house, rendered immortal by the pen of the poet, they have, in straightening the creek, absolutely made three sharp angles to strike the point at which they aimed. Sagacious men! Know they not that "the blood of the martyrs is the seed of the Church?" The name of BARBARA FRITCHIE long shall live after that of those "dressed in a little brief authority" shall have passed away forever. The tuneful nine have it in care, and poetry and song shall waft it down to future ages, and men shall say that WHITTIER wrote when BARBARA lived.

Now that the long, loved, picturesque little house has gone forever, an air of romance and of mystery is thrown around it and its history, which could never have been so long as it stood a material object to the view, and as over the old site the sluggish waters of the creek flow toward the sea, they will yet whisper the name of BARBARA to a free and loyal people. Photographs have been taken of it, and pencils will yet adorn the palace and the cottage, wherever breathes that patriotic love of country of which BARBARA FRITCHIE is the embodiment and her house the standpoint.

On the desk before me I have two photographs, one of the good old woman, the other of the strange old-fashioned house; that of the house is now doubly dear to me, and in a few years will be priceless; the firm yet gentle features of the old lady look on me kindly as a I write, and seem to smile as I make the proposition that a monument on which shall be recorded her patriotism and heroism shall be erected in this city to her memory. On the pedestal might be inscribed:

"Up rose Barbara Fritchie then,
Bowed with her fourscore years and ten,
Bravest of all in Frederick-town;
She took up the flag the men hauled down,
in her attic window the staff she set,
To show that one heart was loyal yet."

Thus did the Romans of their matrons. Let some one more able than I take up this subject, and the necessary money can be raised, if not here, in those parts of the country where honor and patriotism are still held in reverence, and the love for the old flag still burns warm and true.

The damage to the original home from a temporary flood from the creek rising too high was apparently just some damage to the floor boards. It certainly could have been repaired and preserved as a historical landmark. Tourists certainly wanted that as they continued to flock to the site even after it was torn down. The wood from the home was used to make canes to sell as "Barbara Fritchie canes." The comments from local citizens on the true condition of the house vary from some of the Unionists claiming it had minor damage to the floorboards to some of the Southern sympathizers claiming it was nearly washed away from the flood and was not able to be saved. Yet the man who bought it had to hire men to take it down. Many articles were written in a variety of cities pleading for the house to be spared. The author thinks this article above represented how so many felt at the time it was removed.

Published in the New York Times on Oct. 29, 1899, on page 18:

The Real Barbara Frietchie

To the Editor of the New York Times:

You were kind enough to republish on the 13th inst. an article which I sent you apropos of the Barbara Frietchie controversy, and which appeared soon after Whittier's death in The Frederick (MD) Examiner, having been written by Mrs. Shriver Tompkins, now Mrs. Rives of 905 Cathedral Street, Baltimore, who was a friend of Whittier, and also knew Barbara Frietchie personally. I am in possession of a letter written by Mrs. Rives on Monday of this week, which I quote

"The article to which you refer was never intended for publication, but written to a friend in Frederick after my visit to Mr. Whittier. Barbara Frietchie was loyal to her heart's core. This I state from personal knowledge, though I believe she was the only member of her family who was. She was not bedridden at the time of the battles of Antietam and South Mountain, for I saw and conversed with her at that time. She had a small flag which she kept in her window during the memorable week of Gen. Robert E. Lee's occupation of Frederick. Barbara Frietchie was not a myth, neither was her loyalty. I have always understood and believed absolutely that she waved her flag as Gen. Reno passed her house, he looking at her and exclaiming, "The spirit of '76!' I have a beautiful photograph of her in her high white cap and kerchief and dark black or blue gown. My father, the late Gen. Shriver, was an uncompromising Union man, and I knew Mrs. Frietchie personally. There can be no doubt of her loyalty to the old flag."

Since, as Mrs. Rives states, Barbara Frietchie's relatives were not in sympathy with her loyalty to the Union cause, we can understand, perhaps, why the present generation of her people should inform Mr. Clyde Fitch that Barbara would have waved a Confederate flag if she had waved one at all.

Mrs. Rives is a friend of Mrs. Ritchie of Frederick, mother of Mrs. Donald McLean, and in a conversation with Mrs. Ritchie several years ago, she told me that my father, Gen. Reno, and his officers saluted Barbara Frietchie as they marched past her window in September, 1862. He was killed in battle a few hours later.

Jesse W. Reno

No. 347 fifth Avenue, New York, Oct. 25, 1899.

Published April 14, 1900, page 27

BARBARA FRIETCHIE.

Senator Depew Gets Confirmation of the Story.

Washington Dispatch to The New York Sun of April 12. A large delegation from Frederick, Md., appeared before the Committee on Claims of the House and Senate today in behalf of the claim of the City of Frederick for $200,000. The beautiful little town of Frederick, "green walled by the hills of Maryland," occupied rather a conspicuous and unfortunate position during the war. Part of the town was rebel and part Union, and feeling ran high. One summer, it was in 1864, Gen. Jubal A. Early thought to pay a visit to Washington, and as an escort took along some 20,000 to 30,000 veterans. He hoped to give the Federal authorities a surprise party and thought he might be fortunate enough to take possession of the seat of Government. En route, he called at Frederick, and as a souvenir of his visit he suggested to the citizens of that place that they, being loyal sons of the South, should contribute $200,000 toward the support of the Southern Army, and particularly that part of it under his immediate command. As the citizens displayed some reluctance to comply with his request, under threats Gen. Early pressed them, and the householders therefore went down into their strong boxes and the housewives into their stockings and produced the ready money, with which Gen. Early marched away. The delay occasioned by this financial transaction gave Grant time to throw into Washington a part of his army, and when Gen. Early reached the city, instead of finding it guarded only by a few department clerks and convalescents, as he had been led to believe, he found a fair-sized army looking down from well-made breastworks, prepared to give him the warmest reception he could ask. He therefore returned southward without calling on Lincoln or on Congress to refund the $200,000, which they contend not only saved Frederick but the Nation's capital.

It was toward the end of the hearing that Senator Depew drifted into the committee room and took his seat. All the members of the delegation recognized him at once, and whisper ran around the room. "There's Senator Depew." Mr. Depew bowed and smiled at the recognition of his entrance. A few moments later the hearing closed and Mr. Depew blandly remarked: "There is one question which I would like to ask-one which I have long desired to have answered, and which, I think, is of great historical interest. You gentlemen should be able to answer it better than any one else. I refer to the story of Barbara Frietchie."

Immediately half a dozen of the delegation sprang forward. On the poem of Whittier rests Frederick's claim to fame, and no loyal citizen of that burg would think for a moment of denying the truth of the story. So every one of those who volunteered to speak was prepared to swear by all that was good and holy that the poem was as true as the Gospel. The testimony was cumulative. First Col. Goldsborough, a veteran of the war and an old resident of Frederick stepped forward and announced that he had known Barbara Frietchie well, thus establishing the fact of her existence and her identity. Senator McComas of Maryland supplemented this information by the announcement that he had seen the flag itself. At this a murmur of interest and approbation ran around the room. An elderly man, J.C. Hart said that he had known Barbara personally very well. He knew the house and had often seen the flag in the house.

The testimony was getting stronger and stronger. Mr. Hart however, nearly ruined the case when he said he was under the impression that not Barbara, but another woman who lived a few doors away, waved the flag. At this the loyal members of the delegation gave vent to strong expressions of disapproval, and Mr. Hart retired in confusion. Col. Goldsborough then said that he was certain Mrs. Frietchie, who was intensely patriotic, had waved the flag as the Confederates retired from the city. As the Confederates under Jackson slowly retired at the end of the street, the Federals under Burnside entered at the other end of the street. Mrs. Frietchie flung the flag to the breeze as the Confederates withdrew, and the Federals cheered it as they entered the town. An officer on Burnside's staff witnessed the episode and wrote to Whittier about it, and the poet obtained from the Postmaster of Frederick the information on which he based the story.

Senator Depew followed the testimony carefully nodding his head approvingly as each witness gave corroborative evidence. "Barbara Frietchie," he said, "was one of the idols of my childhood. As I played around my mother's knees, and later when I culled wisdom from the school primer, my heart throbbed in sympathy with the old gray-haired woman who so valiantly displayed her patriotism and defied the enemies of her country." The delegation looked aghast at this, but finally reached the conclusion that the Senator had his dates mixed and thought the incident happened during the war of 1812.

Douglas Hargett, Clerk of the County Court, offered the statement that his father had witnessed the episode; had often told him of seeing the old woman, her scanty gray locks floating in the wind, supporting the flag while the Confederate troops marched below. The climax came however, when John H. Abbott announced that his wife had stood with Barbara Frietchie while she waved the flag and that he had the flag at home, framed and hanging on the wall, and invited Senator Depew to come and see it. "That's right," said Senator McComas, "I have seen the flag there myself many times."

There was nothing more to be said. Whittier had been vindicated, Barbara Frietchie had been honored. Senator Depew was delighted at his success in eliciting this valuable information, and with his face wreathed in smiles announced that he for one thought it was worth $200,000 to have this question definitely settled, and that it was probably because of the flag incident and the poem which followed that Early made the city pay the ransom.

Note: Every newspaper article was transcribed as it was originally printed in the paper despite the run-on sentences, old fashioned abbreviations, misspellings and poor grammar.

The newspaper articles supporting both points of view regarding Barbara continue to be written and published for over 160 years since the flag waving occurred.

Notes by the author: One day when the author heard Mrs. Henning's 3rd grade classroom in Bamber Valley Elementary School, Rochester, Minnesota, reciting the poem, Barbara Frietchie, written by John Greenleaf Whittier, she was so proud to tell them that she was related to this brave and patriotic woman. That night she looked for the first time at the Wikipedia page for "Barbara Fritchie" and was shocked to find that the Wikipedia page said Barbara had no children. How could this be? If she truly did not have children, then why has my family passed on this story for six generations? Unfortunately, that Wikipedia page was there during the celebration of the 150th anniversary of the Civil War so while so many were researching the Civil War heroes and heroines, they were given misinformation on this site. There was a domino effect with spreading this rumor. That was only the first feeling of bewilderment; she then was surprised to read an article in The Washington Post about how the reporter was so disappointed to find out that the story of the heroine from his childhood, that of Barbara Fritchie, was just a sham. She was again outraged. She called him to find out what his sources were and, to my surprise, all three of the so-called reliable sources he gave me, stemmed from a single source which happened to be the author of the Wikipedia page. The Wikipedia page was not written by a historical society of the area, or a committee, or a group of historians, but just ONE person who authored this biased Wikipedia page. She called the source of the Wikipedia page and learned that this Frederick, Maryland, local historian said the town did not have much information on Barbara before age 39 except for her place of birth and marriage so it was assumed that because she did not leave anything to children in a will, she had been childless. He also felt because she was 39 when she married that she was too old to have children. She was speechless by this rationale.

(His rationale was an "irrational" opinion!) For this time period, it was a very common practice to not mention a widow or widower's first marriage, and also to never speak of children who may have been disowned. A good example of this happened when the author's own mother who is of 100% German ancestry (like Barbara) was exploring a cemetery where she went with her parents to a relative's funeral. As an elementary school student, she noticed two graves with the same last name as hers, and she did not know whose they were. When she innocently questioned her parents later that day about how she was related, she learned that her own father had been married before and had a son. Both his first wife and son died in the influenza epidemic in Minnesota in 1917. Her father remarried, and, out of respect for his second wife, the author's grandmother, they just never discussed his first wife and son. This was her first marriage. The local Frederick historian sounded so sure (still based on only his "assumptions") that Barbara did not have children, and as the author tried to explain to him her evidence to support her claims, he was quick to dismiss them. Just to verify, she again asked her family at her reunion how sure they were that they were descended from her. Her dad's first cousin, Barbara (Ohslund) Tasa, was quick to respond emphatically stating with a sarcastic grin, "and just who do you think I'm named after?" Yes, she was named after the famous Barbara Fritchie. The author's great grandparents, Maude and LeRoy David Thayer, had a dog named Fritz after Barbara Fritchie because it was also spunky with a mind of its own like Barbara. Maude and LeRoy had four children. The author's grandpa, Ellsworth Albert Thayer, was their youngest child. All of their descendants are also related to Barbara. ...and so the research began

We cannot rewrite the past with our modern day speculations of a historical event.

William Warren Thayer died in a farming accident in Oneida, Wisconsin. He is the son of Albert and Mary (Colburn) Thayer, and brother to LeRoy Thayer. In his obituary, it states that he is the great-grandson of Barbara Fritchie.

When the author asked her dad if he had any "proof" of their lineage to Barbara, he said that it was his grandma Maude who did all the genealogy for the family and documented all of that. Late in life, the author's dad wanted to join The General Society of Mayflower Descendants but found out he needed to have a primary source such as the actual birth, marriage, or death certificate to verify each generation going back to the Mayflower ancestor. When a family line has a generation that already had an approved membership to the Society, then the new member seeking membership only needs to provide their legal documents linking them to the former member. In his line, there were not any previous members who joined the society so every generation had to prove for themselves. The author

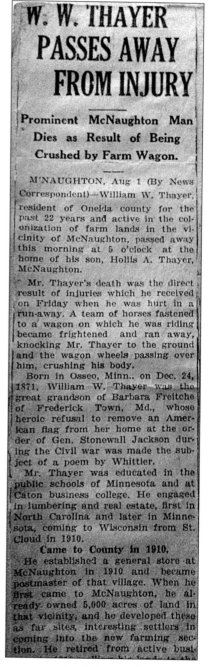

W. W. THAYER PASSES AWAY FROM INJURY

Prominent McNaughton Man Dies as Result of Being Crushed by Farm Wagon.

M'NAUGHTON, Aug 1 (By News Correspondent)—William W. Thayer, resident of Oneida county for the past 22 years and active in the colonization of farm lands in the vicinity of McNaughton, passed away this morning at 5 o'clock at the home of his son, Hollis A. Thayer, McNaughton.

Mr. Thayer's death was the direct result of injuries which he received on Friday when he was hurt in a run-away. A team of horses fastened to a wagon on which he was riding became frightened and ran away, knocking Mr. Thayer to the ground and the wagon wheels passing over him, crushing his body.

Born in Osseo, Minn., on Dec. 24, 1871, William W. Thayer was the great grandson of Barbara Freitche of Frederick Town, Md., whose heroic refusal to remove an American flag from her home at the order of Gen. Stonewall Jackson during the Civil war was made the subject of a poem by Whittier.

Mr. Thayer was educated in the public schools of Minnesota and at Caton business college. He engaged in lumbering and real estate, first in North Carolina and later in Minnesota, coming to Wisconsin from St. Cloud in 1910.

Came to County in 1910.

He established a general store at McNaughton in 1910 and became postmaster of that village. When he first came to McNaughton, he already owned 5,000 acres of land in that vicinity, and he developed these as far sites, interesting settlers in coming into the new farming section. He retired from active busi-

William Warren Thayer
died August 1, 1932.

and her mother spent a few years gathering all those documents, and as a result on September 14, 2012, David Thayer became an official member verifying he is the 12th generation descended from Captain Myles Standish. They are descendants from a few of the pilgrims, but that long process of verification and paper work is required separately for each link so they are happy to have one direct line approved.

This research process hooked the author on genealogy though and after joining The General Society of Mayflower Descendants herself, and working on her Daughters of the American Revolution application at present, She learned a lot of helpful tools to do this kind of research. She presents a variety of workshops on genealogy, and is working hard at putting all the information on both sides of her family into a printed family history book. She has enjoyed the adventure of genealogy research for many years and the process of discovering her own family history. Knowing where one came from can give a better understanding of who one is. Her father was proud of her for gathering all the family documentation required to join the society. He said he regretted that he did not really care about genealogy when his grandmother was alive and so he never asked exactly how he was descended from Barbara Fritchie. He told the author that he had Barbara's picture though, and since she was the one in their family interested in doing research on her and because of her interest in tracing their roots, she could have it. She could not believe he actually had Barbara's picture all this time and did not realize how important this was to their proof of their connection to her.

The author spent years researching Barbara Fritchie and found herself being a sort of detective to prove or disprove her heroics. In this book, she shared what she has uncovered. She hopes, after reading the story of her great great great great grandmother, others too will be inspired to proudly wave our flag with a restored faith in true patriotism.

Barbara Jeannette (Ohslund) Tasa is the third great-granddaughter of Barbara Hauer Fritchie, her name sake. She is pictured here in about the 1940's with her cousin David Thayer (father of the author).

Barbara Fritchie

11

★ THE CONSPIRACY THEORY ★

When Stonewall Jackson showed compassion for an old woman who was a true patriot by ordering his men to not shoot, his change of heart was simply because there was no reason to shoot an innocent woman who was refusing to take down her flag. His men did not see it that way. Immediately after the incident, a couple of his men said it made Jackson look weak and that this would not be good for his reputation as a fearless leader of his rebel army. So they started to plot what to do to discredit the story of what happened. At first they simply denied it happened. After they had a devastating defeat in battle and dragged their feet back through the streets of Frederick, Mary Quantrill waved the flag as she taunted them on the street. This incident clearly happened after Barbara's flag waving. Why would Jackson's men say it was Mary instead of Barbara who waved the flag? Because it causes confusion if people think that two stories may have gotten mixed together or even that one didn't happen. This author believes it is possible they both happened. She believes Mary Quantrill would have been on the confederacy side like her husband's family and his uncle who led the dreadful Quantrill Raiders. She was outspoken against Barbara to discredit her fame. Mary may have been worried when it looked like clearly the North was winning the war when the Southern troops were marching back through Frederick with such defeat after one of the bloodiest battles lost. She may have thought she needed to be a turn-coat at this very moment to be on the winning side. After the Civil War was over, she moved out of state.

After the war, much of Frederick's loyalty was still divided.

The older larger monument says,
"IN MEMORY OF THE YOUNG MEN FROM
FREDERICK COUNTY WHO FOUGHT FOR
SOUTHERN RIGHTS 1861 - 1865."
It lists the names of the Confederate
soldiers from Frederick County.

At Mount Olivet Cemetery they have
preserved the original tombstones and
put a larger replacement one behind the
original ones to honor the Confederate
soldiers who served in the Civil War.
Wouldn't it be great if the same could
be done for the Union Soldiers from
Frederick County someday?

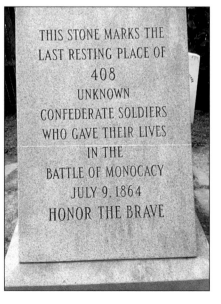

THIS STONE MARKS THE
LAST RESTING PLACE OF
408
UNKNOWN
CONFEDERATE SOLDIERS
WHO GAVE THEIR LIVES
IN THE
BATTLE OF MONOCACY
JULY 9, 1864
HONOR THE BRAVE

The author noticed several Confederate flags like this one on the tall flag pole in the center of the photo displayed by monuments throughout the cemetery but didn't notice the same display of the Union flag.

Whittier's poem:
People asked him if the story was true and he said yes.

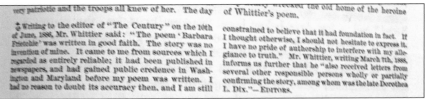

Yet people twisted his own words and claim he meant that he is not sure if it was a true story. His own words clearly say otherwise.

There seems to be more to this cover-up than just trying to protect Jackson's reputation by his loyal followers. The cover-up also seems far more than just Southern sympathizers wanting to discredit a loyal Unionist and Abolitionist. There has been so much effort to debunk her story, that there must be a much greater reason.

One conspiracy theory is that this cover-up against Barbara was used to protect Dr. Ross from any association with Jackson or involvement in the Lost Order 191. Is there another reason mentioned in the "Southern Historical Society Papers" that require Barbara's story to be dismissed as part of another cover-up? Some believe the note that

H. Kyd Douglas first presented years after the fact supposedly written by Jackson and delivered to Dr. Ross by Douglas is a forgery. When one interprets the purpose of the note, it seems clear its only purpose was to give Dr. Ross an alibi that he had not seen Jackson during his stay outside of Frederick from September 5 - 10. It is not written in the type of conversation one would use when writing to a dear friend. If the note was indeed left by Douglas at the home for Dr. Ross, then wouldn't it have remained in the possession of a family member of Dr. Ross over the years and not back in the hands of Douglas? It is written, supposedly, on the back of a paper stock used by Lee's staff. The wording on the reverse side is supposed to be that of Lees's request for more volunteers from Frederick to join their cause. The wording is not a match from the original notice that Lee sent out from his camp, nor is his address on the letterhead spelled correctly. Yet this note has been determined by two writing experts to be authentic. The two experts are Robert K. Krick, a former U.S. Park Service employee, who wrote about the Confederate military, and George Stevenson, Jr., who was employed with the North Carolina State Archives.

They said that it is Jackson's handwriting on the reverse side of Lee's original notice he distributed for recruits. Look at the letter yourself and decide if it looks like the handwriting of Stonewall Jackson:

It reads:

Regret not being permitted to see Dr. & Mrs. Ross, but could not expect to have that pleasure at so unreasonable an hour.

T. J. Jackson
Sept 10/62 5 & 1/4am

***Compare to another example
of Jackson's confirmed
handwriting from 1841***

SPECIMENS OF GENERAL JACKSON'S HANDWRITING.
Being fac-simile extracts from letter at pages 293-4. The
last two reduced.

Written January 26, 1861

Jackson's Handwriting on September 10, 1862

The author of this book is not a writing expert and therefore her comments are admittedly only opinions. In comparing the writing examples that have all been acknowledged as official examples of Jackson's writing, she noticed a few discrepancies. First, look at the difference in how the "T" is varied in Jackson's signatures. The "kson" part of "Jackson" is written at an upward angle only in the note to Dr. Ross. The note to Dr. John B. Ross is written sloppily compared to the neat hand writing in the other examples.

The note states that Jackson never saw Ross during his long stay in Frederick. As stated earlier, Jackson was visiting him so often that the hitching post was named after him. In reality, it was because of this friendship and frequent visits from Jackson that people from his congregation made Dr. Ross feel that he should be careful about with whom he associated. Dr. Ross felt the congregation which was once divided in its loyalties now represented more union supporters, so he resigned. He felt he could no longer serve them with their differences.

Another example of an obvious cover-up is when some people with secession loyalties in Frederick stated that Jackson never even came to town, and, therefore, he could not have gone by Barbara's house. They say that on the day Jackson's men marched past Barbara's house on their way out of town, Jackson took a different route to go by the Rev. John B. Ross's house to leave a note, and then he caught up with his troops down the road past her home. However, when you look at the website of the Presbyterian church, it had the following posted:

"Rev . John B. Ross, M.D., was installed as pastor of the church on November 1, 1857. Shortly thereafter, the Civil War began to affect Maryland, a border state. According to the historian/pastor, the Rev. Thomas Freeman Dixon, "Troublesome times came, especially for those who dwelt along the border line, house was divided against house, brother against brother, and father against son." The Church was no exception, for both the Union and the Confederates sides had their friends and supporters. During the troubled years, **Rev. Ross was**

visited by his personal Presbyterian friend, General Stonewall Jackson, and in 1862 the tree to which Jackson tethered his horse was known as the "Stonewall Jackson Tree" for years to come. In 1862, the work of pastoring became so difficult and discouraging for Dr. Ross that he gave it up."

So if Jackson had these frequent visits with his friend, then why is it contradicted in his note? It seems more like an alibi to give Dr. Ross to disprove any association with Jackson during his stay in Frederick. The note is not consistent with H. Kyd Douglas's other accounts for what happened. Douglas said that Jackson was asking people on the street for directions, (which would have been unlikely at 5:15 a.m. to find so many citizens walking on the streets). According to many witnesses that watched the troops leave on the 10th, it happened after the sun was up and according to Mary Quantrill's story, she was already teaching school with her students present to witness them march by her house.

Another example of the conspiracy theory is the fact that Jackson went to church at the German Reformed Church instead of Dr. Ross's Presbyterian Church. It is a fact that when in Frederick, Jackson often worshiped in the past at the church of his friend Dr. Ross, and he himself was Presbyterian. He would know the service times. According to Douglas, he brought Jackson to that church to find there were no services and so he brought Jackson to the German Reformed church. While in this church, he was witnessed to fall asleep, and so it is well documented that Jackson was indeed at worship in the German Reformed Church. If this was not his denomination, why would he choose to worship there? It seems Jackson wanted to establish distance from his friend Dr. Ross. In their many visits, did Dr. Ross share with the General his frustration with his congregation for not liking his association with the General? Or was the General wanting to show that Dr. John Ross didn't have the opportunity to be a part of the Lost Order 191? Both the note declaring they never saw each other and the fact Jackson never attended his church would mean Dr. Ross never had contact with Jackson and, therefore, couldn't be a part of the famous Lost Order 191. Douglas never knew that there were so many witnesses that saw the two together that week on many occasions.

Joe Ryan in his well researched article, *The Thomas Stonewall Jackson and Reverend Dr. John B. Ross Connection Revisited,* makes the following point, "Assuming the Note is Authentic, What Was Its Purpose? Is Stonewall doing no more with this note than what he did with his brother-in-law, D.H. Hill? In Hill's case Jackson gave him a defense against the charge he lost the order, and in Dr. Ross's, Jackson gave him a defense against the charge they collaborated?"

H. Kyd Douglas tried to use his story as an alibi for Jackson and Ross not seeing each other while in Frederick. Historians have used that information to disprove Barbara's facts, but, ironically, he was referring to the 10th and not the 6th when it happened. The reader must take into consideration the bias for Douglas's accounts written in his book, *I Rode with Stonewall Jackson.* Douglas was a Confederate and, therefore, he wanted to protect the image of his admired General. He may or may not have been trying to also support the cover-up to take away the honor given a Unionist, Barbara Fritchie. He may also have been trying to help give Dr. Ross the alibi that he wasn't around Jackson while they occupied Frederick. The failure here in his attempts was that his story wasn't consistent. Many facts he wrote about originally were not the same in the second version of his book. In his 1886 version, he wrote:

> . . . before we had been in Maryland many hours, one enthusiastic citizen presented Jackson with a gigantic gray mare. . . the next morning when he mounted his new steed and touched her with his spur the. . . beast reared straight into the air, and, standing erect for a moment, threw herself backward, horse and rider rolling upon the ground. The

general was stunned and severely bruised, and lay upon the ground some time. . . He was then <u>placed in an ambulance,</u> where he rode during the day's march. . .

In this version he mentions an ambulance which was never described by any other witness during Jacksons' stay in Frederick. Douglas does not say that he went with Jackson to church on Sunday night. In his later 1940 rendition of his accounts, attending church with the General was now added. Also in the following 1886 version, he does not mention Jackson stopping at Dr. Ross's house to give him the note:

> Early on the 10th Jackson was off. In Frederick he asked for a map of Chambersburg and its vicinity, and made many irrelevant inquiries about roads and localities in the direction of Pennsylvania. . . Having finished this public inquiry, he took me aside, and after asking me about the different fords of the Potomac. . . told me he was ordered to capture the garrison at Harper's Ferry. . .The troops being on the march, the general and staff rode rapidly out of town and took the head of the column. . . .
>
> I was with him every minute of his time he was in that city—he was there only twice. . .

Of course just as Jacob Englebrecht could not witness every event in his town, so is it impossible for Douglas to be with Jackson every minute of the day.

The book, *I Rode With Stonewall*, was published in 1940 by the University of North Carolina Press. This was published 35 years after the death of Douglas. The preface states:

> This book is not a biography nor a history. . . The greater portion was written immediately after the close of the war from diaries I had kept and notes I had made and when my recollection was fresh and youthful. It was then laid aside and about thirty-three years have

passed over it. Now I have been persuaded to rewrite this manuscript. . . I have added somewhat and taken away more freely. . .
April 1899 H.K.D.

On the 5th we crossed the Potomac at White's Ford. . . and started forward in the direction of Frederick. On that march that day a patriotic citizen presented General Jackson with a horse. . . The next morning (the 6th) the General mounted her, and. . . she rose on her hind feet into the air and went backward, horse and rider to the ground. The General was stunned, bruised, and injured in the back. He lay upon the ground for more than half an hour before he was sufficiently recovered to be removed. . . The General was placed in an ambulance in which he rode during the day. . .

On the morning of the 6th, Jackson's command. . . went into camp about Monocacy Junction about three miles short of Frederick. [He did] not go into Frederick that day. . . . Later in the afternoon, the General was called to Lee's tent. . . . When he got back to his tent he did not venture out again <u>until late in the evening</u>.

He did not go to church Sunday morning, but at night he asked Morrison (his cousin) and myself to go to church with him. He rode in an ambulance, we on horseback. . . .

There being no service in the Presbyterian Church, I took him to hear my old friend Dr. Zacharias of the Reformed Church. . . . (But according to his 1886 version, Douglas was not with Jackson inside the Reformed Church.)

At daylight on Wednesday, the 10th, Jackson was in motion. About sunrise (5:41 a.m.) he and his staff rode into Frederick, but early as it was, there were many people in the streets. (If this is so, why would Ross not be up and about also?) He asked <u>his engineer</u> for a map of Chambersburg and enquired of the people the distances to various places

The General was anxious, before leaving Frederick, to see the Rev. Dr. Ross, the Presbyterian clergyman and a personal friend, and I took him to his house. The Doctor was not up yet and the General would not allow me to disturb him by ringing the door bell, but he wrote a brief note and left it with a manservant on the pavement to deliver to him. We then went by the most direct route. . . to the head of the column.

Was the story about the horse and the need for the ambulance fabricated as part of the cover-up? According to Douglas's 1886 story, Douglas did not go inside the Reformed Church. In this new 1940 book, he was a friend of Dr. Zacharias and brought Jackson to worship there. In his first version, Jackson was asking the general public for a map of Chambersburg, but in the 1940 book, he asked his engineer for the map. Why was the General anxious to see the Rev. Dr. Ross, after all, he had already been in town for five days and had every opportunity to see him. Why wait until he needed to leave town? There are many other examples that show things were added or deleted from the original manuscript.

In summarizing the conspiracy, the author believes that the note from Jackson to Dr. Ross was created after the fact to either debunk Barbara's story and protect the image of Jackson, or it was created for a much bigger conspiracy that has yet to be revealed.

J. Thomas Scharf authored the book, *The History of Western Maryland, in 1882*. He mentions that on Sunday, September 7, Jackson attended services at both the Presbyterian Church and the Reformed Church. He also states the following about the Barbara Fritchie and Stonewall incident.

confronting the Barbara Freitchie myth.

(1) As to the *time*. Unfortunately for Mr. Whittier, he indicates that in a very precise way. "Forty flags," he tells us, "flapped in the morning wind,"—at noon "not one." It was high noon, therefore, upon his hypothesis, when old Barbara Freitchie rose and hung out her flag. As a rule, persons of Mrs. Freitchie's age, as Mr. Whittier has forgotten, are the earliest risers. Still, she might have overslept herself upon this particular occasion, so momentous to the extremely loyal. If she had been awake, as it is presumable she was, at a peculiarly early hour of the dawn, say 5.15 A.M., she would have seen "Stonewall" Jackson "riding ahead" in front of "the rebel horde." That was the hour when it is alleged he passed by her house, and of that particular fact we have explicit evidence, presently to be produced. At 5.15 A.M. on Sept. 15, 1862, the "Hagerstown Almanac" tells us, the sun was about twenty-five minutes below the horizon, and consequently, unless the morning twilight was particularly clear and bright (which it seldom is, even on high ground, until at least a month later, and probably never is in the valley of the Monocacy), it would have been very hard to see a large flag, much less a little one, at that hour. That particular minute, however, was the one of "Stonewall" Jackson's passing. Proof: an autograph note of Jackson's, written impromptu nearest the point to which he came in passing through that neighborhood,—a note addressed to his friend Mrs. Ross, a daughter of Governor McDowell, of Virginia, which reads like a drum-head message, to wit:

"Regret not being permitted to see Dr. and Mrs. Ross, but could not expect to have that pleasure at so unseasonable an hour.

"T. J. JACKSON.

"SEPT. 10, 1862, 5¼ A.M"

This ought to satisfy all doubters.

But other proof is behind. Jackson and his command were by no means moving on the route Mr. Whittier gives them to

Maj. H. Kyd Douglas, now a leading member of the Hagers-town bar, and who was during the late war on Gen. "Stonewall" Jackson's staff, says,—

"Jackson's corps crossed the Potomac into Maryland Sept. 5, 1862, and on that day an admiring civilian of Western Maryland presented the general with a large gray horse. The next morning, when he tried to ride him, he became unmanageable, and in rearing fell backward upon the general, who was so severely hurt that it was some time before he sufficiently recovered to be moved. He was then placed in an ambulance, and turned his command over to Gen. D. H. Hill. Jackson stopped about three miles short of Frederick, and established his headquarters in Best's Grove, as also did Gens. Lee and Longstreet. He did not go into Frederick that day, and certainly was not 'riding ahead' of the 'rebel tread' which passed through Frederick to the other side. While encamped near Frederick he kept closely to his tent, seeing very few of the many citizens who called on him. On Sunday night he asked Majs. Douglas and Morrison of his staff to go to church with him, and was taken to town in an ambulance. There being no service in the Presbyterian church, he went to hear Dr. Zacharias at the Evangelical Reformed church, and, as usual, went to sleep. On the morning of the 10th Jackson's corps was put in motion, and the general went to Frederick in an ambulance, and then mounted his horse. While the army was passing through, he rode with Maj. Douglas to the house of Dr. Ross, the Presbyterian pastor, and left a note for him with a servant, with instructions to deliver when the doctor got up, but not to awake him for the purpose. This being

Douglas's story states Jackson mounts a horse <u>in</u> Frederick. Scharf, in his 1882 book, also states, without providing a source, that, on Sunday, September 7th, Jackson attended services at both the Presbyterian Church and the Reformed Church.

Century Magazine, in 1886, printed a rebuttal with Douglas's denial of the flag waving.

On Sunday the churches were opened as usual, and were filled with Confederate officers and soldiers. Gen. Jackson attended the Presbyterian and German Reformed churches. On Monday, September 8th,

It is interesting to note that Barbara's nieces were asked to speak at many events about the actions of Barbara. One event took place in New York City. Douglas arrived after they left and in, April 1900, Douglas spoke at Cooper Union in New York City counteracting the story as it was just told by Barbara's family.

Vol. 16.   Concord Junction, April 28, 1900.   No. 17.

The Legend of Barbara Frietchie

The legend of Barbara Frietchie was badly damaged in an address on "Stonewall" Jackson, delivered at Cooper union New York, April 23, by Gen Henry Kyd Douglas, an officer on Gen. Jackson's staff. Gen. Douglas told what he says is the true story of "Stonewall's entry into Frederick.

"Gen. Jackson never even passed Barbara Frietchie's house." said Gen. Douglas. "It seems hard to believe that all that beautiful poem is fiction, but the fact remains. Not even her relatives will sanction the story.

"Gen. Jackson, just before our entry into Frederick, had been seriously injured by a fall from a horse that had been presented to him by some of his admirers. We were obliged to place Gen. Jackson in an ambulance and stop at Best's Grove, about three miles from Frederick.

"Gen Jackson, on the following Sunday evening, insisted on being taken into Frederick in the ambulance to attend church. He did not return to town again until the morning of the supposed incident, Sept 10, 1862. Then we again took him into town in the ambulance.

"We stopped at the corner of Patrick and Main streets and there he asked some of the citizens misleading questions about the surrounding country. Then he directed that I drive with him to the residence of Rev. Dr. Ross, the Presbyterian clergyman, whose church we had attended on the preceding Sunday evening. It was still so early that Dr. Ross was not up, so we left a card.

"We drove the ambulance past the present court house, past the home of William Bantz, then down Mill alley to Middletown pike, when we reached Jackson's column and rode up to the front. We did not pass Barbara Frietchie's house.

"Barbara Frietchie, I have learned, after long and painstaking investigation, was 96 years old at that time. She was helpless and almost blind. No soldier of our army or resident of Frederick saw a flag at her window. Her relatives, with whom I have talked, admit that there is no foundation for the story on which Whittier has written such a beautiful poem."

After the publication of Whittier's poem both Anna, Jackson's widow, and his daughter thanked Whittier for describing Jackson in a kind way as he had defended and allowed Barbara's flag waving actions to continue. They believed the story and thought it showed his compassion. Sometime after that, however, Anna is supporting Douglas's statements that Jackson never had contact with Barbara. Mysteriously in this book published in 1901 both Douglas and Jackson's widow have changed their story accounts. Here Jackson attended Sunday service at Dr. Ross's church according to Douglas.

STORY OF

STONEWALL JACKSON.

A NARRATIVE

OF THE

Career of Thomas Jonathan (Stonewall) Jackson, From
Written and Verbal Accounts of His Life.
Approved by His Widow,

MARY ANNA JACKSON.

ATLANTA, GA.:

D. E. LUTHER PUBLISHING COMPANY,

1901.

She leaned far out on window sill,
And shook it forth with a royal will.
'Shoot, if you must, this old gray head
But spare your country's flag,' she said.
A shade of sadness, a blush of shame
Over the face of the leader came:
The nobler nature within him stirred

To life at that woman's deed and word.
'Who touches a hair of yon gray head,
Dies like a dog! March on,' he said.

* * * * * *

Honor to her! And let a tear
Fall, for her sake, on Stonewall's bier."

Alas, for the poet! That rude hands should have to sweep away this dramatic fabrication, which his many admirers have so long regarded as drawn from life. But we have been told by members of General Jackson's staff that this pretty story was a fabrication. This is confirmed by Dame Barbara's own nephew, Valerius Ebert, of Frederick City, Maryland, who writes as follows to a Northern paper :

"As to the waving of the Federal flag in the face of the rebels by Dame Barbara on the occasion of Stonewall Jackson's march through Frederick, truth requires me to say that Stonewall Jackson with his troops did not pass Barbara Frietchie's residence at all, but passed through what in this city is called "The Mill Alley," about three hundred yards from her residence, then passed due west towards Antietam, and thus out of the city. But another and still stronger fact with regard to this matter may be here presented, namely, the poem by Whittier represents our venerable relative (then ninety-six years of age) as nimbly ascending to her attic window and waving her small Federal flag defiantly in the face of Stonewall Jackson's troops. Now, Dame Barbara was at the moment bed-ridden and helpless and had lost the power of locomotion. She could at that period only move, as she was moved, by the help of her attendants. These are the facts,

Dr. Steiner was the first to mention anything about a note but stated he witnessed Jackson leave a note for Dr. Ross early on September 6. The note stated he would see his friend at church the next day. Dr. Steiner was one of many witnesses to see Jackson attend Ross's church. Historians have found many examples of Douglas changing the facts of his story as he publicly spoke on the subject and from comparing his first printed version to the second version of his book printed after his death by his nephew. It seems as witnesses disputed Douglas's story he created more details and evidence to support his story forgetting what he had previously stated on the matter, leaving him an unreliable source on the incident, based on this author's opinion.

The first typewriters were invented just after the Civil War in about 1870. In 1857, the Hood Typewriter, was invented for a blind man to print one letter of the alphabet at a time with the letters on a wheel that needed to be rotated to line up each letter. It seems more likely that when General Lee printed his famous letter to recruit the men in Maryland to join the cause, he used a newspaper printing press and therefore all the copies printed would be identical. Although a typewriter time-consuming prototype was in operation, the assertion that the typewriter was used by a Civil War general is controversial and unlikely. The original authentic copy of this document is located in the Official Records of the Rebellion on page 601 of Vol 19. The note to Dr. Ross from Jackson that Douglas first materializes years later, is written on the reverse side of Lee's letter. This may have been

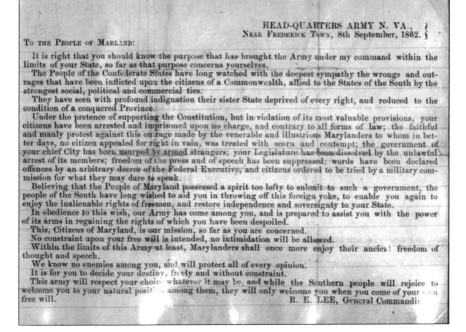

General Lee's letter to recruit the people of Maryland.

an attempt to make the Dr. Ross letter look more authentic, using paper that may have been available at the time. However, the typeset of the heading doesn't match the authentic one in the Official Records of the Rebellion. The wording does not match and there are errors in Douglas's copy. And if this letter was actually left for Dr. Ross, how did it get back to Douglas years later? With Dr. Ross wanting to distance himself from Jackson at this time, he would have destroyed the letter? The author is not an expert to judge the authenticity of the letter, but points out to the reader that the letter first shows up when Douglas needs evidence to support his claim, after typewriters are invented. Or was a printing press used years later to possibly make a poor attempt at a forgery?

A summary of a letter to the Editor of the New York Times written by Edgar S. Thomson on Nov. 8, 1927 states that he heard this story from Miss Eleanor D. Abbott the great-grandniece of Barbara. "Stonewall marched through Frederick on Sept. 5, 1862. Barbara's sympathies were always strongly with the Union, and she would at times speak very sharply to the Confederate soldiers who passed the door of her house on Patrick Street. On Sept. 6 it was evident that something had occurred to disturb her, but it was not until a month later that she finally told her niece, Mrs. Hanshaw, what had actually occurred. Hearing the troops were approaching she took her silk flag from between the leaves of the family Bible, and stepped out on her front porch, thinking they were Union soldiers. Immediately an officer rode up, saying 'Granny, give me your flag.' 'You can't have it.' She said, and then noticed the gray uniforms, but she continued waving. He spoke to the men, and they turned, facing her. She thought they meant to fire on her, but instead, he rode on a short distance to the Mill Alley, returning in a moment with another officer and some men. This officer said to her, 'Give me your flag, Granny, and I'll stick it in my horses's head.' 'No, you can't have it,' she said. One of the men called out, 'Shoot her damned head off.' The officer turned angrily upon him, saying, 'If you harm a hair of her head I'll shoot you down like a dog.' Then, turning to the trembling old lady, he said, 'Go on, Granny, wave your flag as much as you please.'" ...Miss Abbott received several letters from men who were in the Confederate ranks confirming her story.

Another example of this whole conspiracy theory is the great lengths taken to discredit a respected Unionist and Abolitionist by people who were southern sympathizers. Some went as far as to say she never existed, others said she was a person but was bed ridden, and others tried to say she owned slaves and never had children. Do not forget the haste of a southerner to take down Barbara's house after the floor boards were damaged in a flood. These attempts to wipe her memory from the hearts of the American people who believed in her and admired her have failed. Thanks to the insistence of witnesses, her friends, family, and neighbors her story has been passed on generation to generation. With gratitude to John Greenleaf Whittier she has forever been immortalized as a true patriot!

All three flags that Barbara owned were preserved. This flag Jackson's men shot was framed behind glass and kept by Mrs. Abbott with her other artifacts.

Barbara's grandnieces pose after her monument was erected on September 8, 1914.

12

★ CLUES FROM THE AUTHOR ★
TO SOLVE THE MYSTERIES

My opinion on why Barbara's mysteries may never be solved is because, even though the war ended in 1865, there is still observed bitterness and division in this part of the country that has been carried down to the current generation.

It is upsetting to the author that, at the time the bodies of both John and Barbara Fritchie were removed and reinterred at Mount Olivet Cemetery, the casket of Barbara was allowed to be opened and her personal belongings were taken out. It is hard for the author to prove her DNA match to any hair that may be on Barbara's hair comb if it has been touched by others at the time it was placed in the museum and then moved a few times.

After over 160 years since the Civil War the author has seen there is still rivalry between the North and South such as observed with the fight over the Virginia Battle flag of the 28th Infantry. Here is a glimpse into their ongoing battle.

William Sherman, considered a Minnesota hero, had captured the flag in battle on the third and last day of Gettysburg and received a medal of honor for his duty. The Battle of Gettysburg was July

William Sherman of Minnesota stands by his captured Virginia flag.

1-3, 1863. Sherman was part of the First Minnesota Regiment.[16] The regiment is best known for their stedfast charge at the battle of Gettysburg. With great bravery and determination, the regiment attacked Wilcox's Alabama Brigade in the evening of July 2, 1863, as Wilcox was preparing for the final push to break the Union line. Confederate General Wilcox wrote in his report, "This stronghold of the enemy, together with his batteries, were almost won, when still another line of infantry descended the slope in our front at a double-quick, to the support of their fleeing comrades and for the defense of the batteries." The line of infantry he was referring to was the First Minnesota. Despite the 1:5 ratio they crossed over 200 yards of open ground and relentlessly charged the Confederates. The rebels having the upper hand in numbers with five times that of the Union rebounded which killed or wounded over 170 of the 300 plus men. The survivors of the 1st Minnesota did not panic or give up in the dire circumstances but, instead, fell back to their original position and rallied around the flag waiting for a counterattack that did not come. On July 3, two of the

---

[16] His regiment's history: When President Abraham Lincoln called for 75,000 troops in April, 1861, The First Minnesota Infantry Regiment was one of the first units organized. The regiment was formed immediately by eager men from all parts of Minnesota who wanted to defend the Union of the United States. They received training and reported for duty under Colonel Gorman. By July, 1861, the regiment was sent to battle and fought with distinction at the battle of Bull Run also known as the Battle of Manassas in Virginia. This battle was a confederate victory. This regiment participated in all the major campaigns of the Army of the Potomac through the fall of 1863. The reduced remnant of this regiment fought as skirmishers at the battle of Bristoe Station and mustered out in May,1864. Most of those men including the First Battalion reenlisted and saw heavy action at Petersburg and Appomattox. Appomattox was the final battle of the war. After Sherman was mustered out in May, 1864, he returned to Minnesota where the picture was taken of him standing in front of the captured Virginian flag. He reenlisted and during battle in Petersburg, VA. He was severely wounded above the knee and lost a leg.

First Minnesota Regiment soldiers would earn the medal of honor. The first was to O'Brian who led the charge carrying the colors and despite being shot twice, he never let the flag fall or let the flag be taken by the Confederates. Although the three-day Gettysburg bloody battle was declared a Union victory, it was at a cost of over 85% of the First Minnesota Regiment. For this very reason the captured Virginia flag is a trophy of victory, a tangible remnant of a battle hard fought, and a visual remembrance of the sacrifice of the loyal lives of these brave Minnesota soldiers. It is a symbol of pride and accomplishment for all Minnesotans. After the war the flag appeared in many different places around Minnesota. In 1887, President Grover Cleveland issued an executive order stating all captured flags from the Civil War should be returned to their regiments. This caused much debate and disagreement on both sides. Jefferson Davis, the former president of the Confederate States of America said that the banners belong to the captors, by all known military precedents. President Cleveland rescinded his declaration. Virginia asked Minnesota to return their flag on several occasions since the war ended, but it just meant, too much to Minnesotans to give up their valued trophy. In 2000, Chris Caveness, a Roanoke resident originated a federal lawsuit to get the flag back in Virginia. He worked with the former Virginia Attorney General Anthony Troy and a group of Richmond Law School students to prepare his 45-page legal opinion based on a 1905 act of Congress allowing the return of Confederate flags in possession of the War Department. He suggests that federal property cannot be abandoned or disposed without Congressional assent and since Congress never gave the flag away he believes Minnesota is illegally in possession of the flag. This litigation did not end in action.

Early in 2010, the Virginia Governor Bob McDonnell asked Minnesota to loan the flag to them to celebrate April, 2010, as "Confederate History Month" at the behest of the sons of Confederate Veterans. And the Minnesota Governor Mark Dayton appropriately responded:

The governor of Virginia earlier this year requested that the flag be loaned, quote, unquote, to Virginia to commemorate -- it doesn't quite strike me as something they would want to commemorate, but we declined that invitation. It was taken in a battle at the cost of the blood of all these Minnesotans, and I think it would be a sacrilege to return it to them. It was something that was earned through the incredible courage and valor of men who gave their lives and risked their lives to obtain it. And as far as I'm concerned, it's a closed subject.

The flag remains "one of the true treasures of the Minnesota Historical Society," as their website declares. The author believes this continued battle over the possession of the flag is just one example of many skirmishes still happening today over lingering differences between the north and south.

The genealogy research was done a few generations ago and passed on to the author. This is the "Chase to Thayer" family line. Notice #9 once again mentions Mary Colburn was born February 3, 1850, probably at or near Corning, New York. She was the daughter of Daniel and Barbara (Fritchie) Colburn.

There are additional clues in this book that Barbara really stood up to Jackson's men and waved the flag defiantly. The DNA is proof that the author is a descendant to Barbara. The obituary of her great grandson that lists Barbara as his great grandma is very compelling. And the picture of her passed down through the generations is also proof of her family connection.

Based on Grandma Maude's research, this was typed out and given to the author's father in the 1960's. It mentions Barbara Fritchie Colburn. There was a typo spelling Mary's son's middle name as Leroy instead of LeRoy and she typed "Fritshie" instead of "Fritchie".

1. WILLIAM CHASE of Roxbury and Yarmouth, Mass. came from England to settle at Roxbury Mass. in 1630 in the fleet that brought Gov. Winthrop. As he married in England, he was probably born before 1600, probably around 1595. He was the first of the Chase name to settle in New England. After a few years at Roxbury he moved his family to Yarmouth where his name appears often in the records. He was a carpenter by trade. His will shows that he had considerable property. He had three children of which one was,

2. BENJAMEN CHASE of Freetown Mass. and Portsmouth R.I. He was a cooper by trade and is often mentioned in Plymouth records. as surveyor, constable and selectman. He was born in Roxbury, April 18, 1652. and married about 167 Phillippa Sherman, daughter of Phillip and Sarah (Odding) Sherman. He died at Freetown in 1730 or 1731. He had six children of which one was,

3. Bengamen CHASE born at Freetown July 15, 1682. Died at Westerly, R.I. He married at Tauriton Mass. June 23, 1703 Mercy Simmons. He died in 1767. They had eight children of which one was,

4. CAPT. OLIVER CHASE born at Freetown, Mass. Sept. 23, 1709, died at Westerly R.I. Nov. 14, 1786. He married at Portsmouth, R.I. March 22, 1734. Elizabeth Cleveland, daughter of John and Martha (Simmons) Cleveland. His title shows that he was evidently a sea captain. They had eleven children of which one was,

5. Abner Chase born in Westerly, R.I. Oct. 7, 1745. He married Sarah Elliot and settled on Quaker Hill, Pawling, Dutchess Co. N.Y. just before the Revolution. There his children were born. After the Revolution he moved to Delhi, Deleware Co. N.Y. where he and his wife died. they had six children. the oldest was,

6. Elliot CHASE born Jan. 10, 1772. In 1795 he married Thirza Rogers, daughter of Cabel and Azuba (Foster) Rogers, and settled at Paris, Oneida Co. N.Y. where all his children were born. Later he with his family moved to Andover, Allegany Co. N.Y. and then to Knoxville, Ill. where he died Sept. 23, 1869. His son Caleb Chase (my mothers father) remained behind at Andover, N.Y. where my mother was born, also myself. Elliots oldest child was,

7. Mary CHASE born at Paris N.Y. Oct. 9, 1797. She married Solomon Warren in 1830 and when the rest of the family migrated to Ill. they went overland and settled near Adrian Mich. Later she and her husband went to Kentland Ind. and then to Kansas where they died. They had four children, of which one was,

8. CATHERINE WARREN born Sept. 17, 1824 and married April 5, 1846 David B. Thayer. Both she and her husband died in Osseo, Minn. They had four children the oldest being

9. ALBERT AGUSTAS THAYER born in Adrian, Mich. Dec. 28, 1848. He came with his parents to Minn. in 1854. In 1864 he enlisted as musician in the 7" Minnesota Vol. Inf. Was mustered out Aug. 16, 1865. In 1870 he — July 5", he married Mary Colburn. She was born Feb. 2, 1850. Probably at or near Corning, N.Y. She was the daughter of Daniel and Barbara (Fritchie) Colburn. They had two children, William Warren Thayer and David Leroy.

10. DAVID LEROY THAYER was born Nov. 4" 1873, at Osseo, Minn. He married Maude Allana Cooper of Fair Haven, Minn. Sept. 2" 1891. She was the daughter of William and Lizzie (Noyes) Cooper. David Leroy Thayer died in Minneapolis April 16, 1930. They had four children.

Chase to Thayer family line

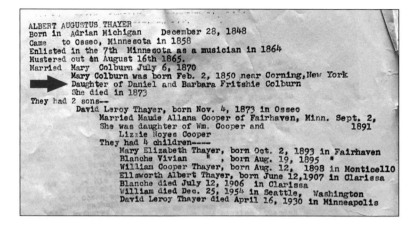

ALBERT AUGUSTUS THAYER
Born in Adrian Michigan   December 28, 1848
Came   to Osseo, Minnesota in 1858
Enlisted in the 7th Minnesota as a musician in 1864
Mustered out on August 16th 1865.
Married Mary Colburn July 6, 1870
➤   Mary Colburn was born Feb. 2, 1850 near Corning, New York
      Daughter of Daniel and Barbara Fritshie Colburn
      She died in 1873
They had 2 sons--
      David Leroy Thayer, born Nov. 4, 1873 in Osseo
      Married Maude Allana Cooper of Fairhaven, Minn. Sept. 2,
      She was daughter of Wm. Cooper and   1891
            Lizzie Noyes Cooper
      They had 4 children----
      Mary Elizabeth Thayer, born Oct. 2, 1893 in Fairhaven
      Blanche Vivian   "   , born Aug. 19, 1895 "
      William Cooper Thayer, born Aug. 12, 1898 in Monticello
      Ellsworth Albert Thayer, born June 12,1907 in Clarissa
      Blanche died July 12, 1906 in Clarissa
      William died Dec. 25, 1954 in Seattle, Washington
      David Leroy Thayer died April 16, 1930 in Minneapolis

Note: This Barbara is the daughter of Barbara (Hauer) Fritchie of Frederick Town, MD.

These clues answer the current charge by one local Frederick historian who claims Barbara and John were hypocrites who claimed to be abolitionists while owning slaves. This new accusation comes 150 years after her death, and she is not here to defend herself. The historian has changed not only her historical markers to read that she was a slave owner, but he has exaggerated on a tourist app that Barbara owned several slaves. An abolitionist with slaves? What does not add up is that some people living in her time period have stated in various resources that Barbara was indeed a very outspoken abolitionist and did not have any slaves.

The author has discovered several reliable sources who have determined Barbara's story to be true, but with so many false stories from southern sympathizers still believed today, it is hard to prove her earned patriotism. Here is one example found in the Lancaster County Historical Society Papers:

It is worthy of note that Dr. Hendel, on December 14, 1766, in the First Reformed Church in Lancaster, baptized an eleven-days-old babe as Barbara Hauer, daughter of Nicholas and Catherine Hauer, members of the congregation. Barbara Hauer, when a woman, married John C. Fritchie, and in her old age was the central figure in a dramatic incident of the Civil War. She was the Barbara Fritchie, immortalized by Whittier, and although some persons later have endeavored to show that Whittier's bases for his poem were imaginary, Judge John H. Landis has pointed to newspaper articles of the time, and of the place, and prior to the writing of the poem, which clearly prove that Barbara Fritchie, a native of Lancaster, is truly entitled to the place that Whittier has accorded her in American history[17].

It is the author's opinion that Barbara's mysteries will never be solved because, even though the war ended April 9, 1865, there is still bitterness and division in this area that has been carried down to the current generation. A simple proof of this is the fact that, for years, the Sons of the Confederacy and the Confederate Daughters groups held their monthly meetings in the Barbara Fritchie restaurant. They could have met anywhere in Frederick, but the very fact that this is the restaurant they chose shows their spite and bitterness against her legacy. The division is shown in a history tour in Frederick where the tone of the guides is very pro-South. There is wonderful preservation of the Confederate artifacts around town, but only a few items preserved representing the North. Even when presented with undeniable facts of Barbara's heroism, some of the locals chose to argue and deny without any contrary proof. The author is hoping historians will discover more facts to expose the conspiracy theory and prove Barbara's true act of patriotism.

---

[17] Lancaster County Historical Society Papers, Vol. XXIII, No. 5.

Barbara Fritchie House

13

★ BARBARA'S LEGACY CONTINUES ★
TO INSPIRE PATIOTISM

Whittier's intent for the poem was to inspire the Union to rally and win the Civil War to keep the country united. He probably never dreamed that it would be so inspirational for generations to come. It inspires patriotism in the reader; after all, if an old woman can stand up for what's right, then surely others can do their part, too. Students had to memorize this poem as part of their curriculum. It was memorized as part of lessons on either Whittier and poetry, or for lessons on government and patriotism.

Many things have been named in her honor. In 1866, a schooner named *Barbara Frietchie*[18], was built in Kennebunk, Maine. It was sailing through 1898. In 1880, a two masted schooner named Barbara Fritchie was wrecked. In 1888, a 127 foot steam schooner was named Barbara Frietchie and was grounded in 1892. There may have been more than these three schooners named in her honor.

The bodies of both John and Barbara Fritchie were removed from their resting place near their friends and family who were also buried

---

[18] This schooner is listed in the book *Civil Merchant Vessel Encounters with United States Navy Ships, 1800-2000* by author Greg H. Williams, page 75.

at the old Reformed Church Graveyard in 1913. At this time their original headstones were also moved to mark their graves until the Barbara Fritchie Memorial Association finished making a monument to be placed at their new gravesite. A big ceremony was held when they were reinterred at Mt. Olivet Cemetery.

The plaque in the picture is mounted on the outside wall of the Barbara Fritchie House and Museum in Frederick, Maryland.

During WWII on May 17, 1943, Sir Winston Churchill was traveling with Franklin D. Roosevelt on their way from "Shangri-La" to Washington D.C., and Churchill asked to stop at Barbara's house. He was able to recite her entire poem from memory which impressed Roosevelt. Shangri-La was the nickname for the meeting place in the Catoctin Mountains which later officially became known as Camp David. The mountains there provide a peaceful and secluded area close to the nation's capital for the Presidents to hold a retreat. These mountains are close to Frederick, Maryland, and were the same ones mentioned earlier in the book where President George Washington would meet. It was in a house in these mountains where Barbara Fritchie and several women were rumored to work, formerly located in or by Camp David. The other mentioned house used as a tavern was in the same mountain range outside of Frederick, MD, and en route to the nation's capitol.

The 4th of July week-long celebrations held in Elysian, Minnesota, are examples of pride. To show their pride in America, they proudly display 50 American flags along the bike trail of this small town of

726, (as of 2017 records). For the 4th of July, they celebrate with a wide variety of activities for an entire week.

In 1990, there was the United States v. Eichman (496 U.S. 310) – Passage of the Flag Protection Act resulting in a number of flag burning incidents protesting the new law. The news showed protesters burning the American flag, and that disrespect was so upsetting to the author. When it was time for the 4th of July kiddie parade in Elysian, she just had to make a statement. So while other young children were dressed in red, white, and blue clothes to march in the parade, her three year old daughter marched dressed in a "Super Baby" costume resembling Superman waving her flag with a sign that said, "Super Baby says DON'T BURN MY FLAG!" Of course the author realizes her daughter had no choice in the political statement she was making on her mom's behalf, but she still must have felt such pride as she waved that flag and saw the crowd cheer her on and respond by clapping for the statement she made. One is never too young to learn to have pride in the flag and to know this is something so special.

In 1911, the Barbara Fritchie Restaurant opened in Frederick. Over the years, it was under different owners with different menus and products or Barbara souvenirs from time to time such as post cards of her house, Barbara Fritchie candy, etc. In 2016, the author and her mother had the pleasure of enjoying their famous Barbara Fritchie pies. They met this new owner and explained how they were descendants of Barbara. He said she would have rolled over in her grave if she knew what was happening in a restaurant named after her. It seems for many years under previous ownership, a group would meet there in a private dining room area and display the Confederate flag and hold their meetings. The new owner gave them their flag back, and they discontinued meeting there. Despite excellent food and great new friendly owners, the restaurant closed on January 1, 2018. It would be great if someone will reopen the restaurant to keep alive this Frederick landmark after serving the community there for 107 years.

The Barbara Fritchie Classic is a motorcycle race held every year at the Frederick Fairgrounds over the 4th of July. It is the oldest running dirt track race in America having started in 1923, and it is named in Barbara's honor.

Barbara Fritchie is a silent film movie with the first version in 1915 and a second version in 1924 about an old woman who helps out soldiers during the Civil War. It is based on the play and only mentioned here because it was named after the same Barbara in this book but doesn't follow her real life story. The playwright took liberties to take her story and combine it into the story of his own grandparents and really has little to do with the real story of Barbara Fritchie.

The Barbara Fritchie Handicap is an American race for thoroughbred horses which is held annually at Laurel Park Racecourse in Laurel, Maryland. Their race was inaugurated in 1952 at Bowie Race Course until being moved to Laurel in 1985. It is named in honor of Barbara Fritchie, and there is a good description of her actions on their website.

In WWII, a liberty ship was named SS Barbara Frietchie built in Baltimore, Maryland in 1943 and was 7,176 gross tons.

The original flag that had been shot through by Jackson's men was on display at the Frederick museum. When attempts were made to locate it, workers said it was placed in storage in a back room. The smaller silk flag that Barbara gave Reno heading into battle was brought back with his body and eventually put in a museum. The note supposedly left by Stonewall Jackson to Dr. Ross was sold at auction.

The Frederick Historical Society Museum on 24 Church Street in Frederick, MD, has Barbara's chair and desk on display.

| *Barbara Fritchie Windsor Chair* | *Barbara Fritchie Desk* |

This Windsor chair dates from 1800 to 1825. Oral tradition from the descendants of Barbara Fritchie has it that it sat in her house. With stylistic elements similar to Pennsylvania Windsor chairs, it could have been made in Pennsylvania and brought to Frederick County by her husband John, whose family lived there. Or a local chair maker could have been influenced by his fellow craftsmen just across the state line.

Donated by Regina Rodock Raggi

The desk made of figured cherry with yellow pine secondary, was purchased by Jabob Byerly from Barbara Frichie's niece. The maker of the desk is unknown, but it may have been made in Frederick County, given its connection to Frederick families. The desk is also constructed of local woods. The lamb's tongue molding is a stylistic element found on Frederick County furniture, and the desk bears similarities to the Englebrecht desk.

Donated by Sissy Rothwell and Barbara Riley

The Frederick, Maryland Visitors Center has a good display about Barbara. Because of the misinformation circulating, some of the signs say that historians have "disproved her story". The signs outside the Barbara Fritchie home also say that historians have disproved her story. Look at the difference between those two and the one posted by her grave at Mount Olivet. At Mount Olivet, the sign just states the facts and doesn't say that the historians have disproved anything because that is just one of the very opposing points of view. Hopefully, the signs at both the Frederick Visitors Center and the AirBnB will change to once again state facts, not opinions. **Barbara waved the flag. She was a patriot. She was an abolitionist. She loved her country. That sums up the facts that should be displayed by her landmarks.**

The Barbara Fritchie AirBnB

Signage from outside of the Barbara Fritchie AirBnB

The entire sign at Mount Olivet.　　　*Close-up view of sign at Mount Olivet.*

Close-up view of sign at Mount Olivet.

14

★ PATRIOTISM AND THE FLAG; ★ LET YOURSELF BE INSPIRED!

Patriotism is to have a deep love of one's country or homeland; a feeling of attachment and pride of one's country; commitment and devotion toward its success, and support and obligation in the country's welfare; willingness to serve for the betterment of and even sacrifice one's own life to protect the country; including an alliance with other citizens who share the same patriotic sentiment. This patriotism is demonstrated by waving flags, standing up at attention and putting the right hand over the heart when the color guard marches by in a parade, standing for the Pledge of Allegiance, singing patriotic songs, decorating with patriotic symbols, and celebrating the national patriotic holidays. Anything that is done to celebrate or make a country stronger is a great way to show patriotism. When those who serve the country are supported by the citizens, it shows the country's patriotism. There are many ways to show support to those who served, are serving, or will serve the country. When all citizens support them, it strengthens the whole country.

The flag may be made out of just fabric but, with a specific design and use of colors, it becomes a *patriotic symbol* of the country it represents. It is used for identification on the battlefield. The flag is displayed in every classroom, courtroom and public building in America. It has its own law and code that must be followed. Its use can show the conquering of a land or winning a battle when it is the first to be posted in that location. The Olympics use the flag raising at the medal ceremony to show pride in the country which achieved athletic victory by putting the winning country's flag above the others. The first country to land on the moon proudly posted the flag. The first country to reach the highest mountain top posts their country's flag there. In war, the military has sacrificed their lives to protect their country's flag and to prevent it from falling into the hands of the enemy.

The following are just a few examples of patriots who have shown true bravery and patriotism in protecting their flag or capturing the flag of their enemy:

1. The first African-American to receive the medal of honor in the Civil War was Sergeant **William Harvey Carney** who was shot in the face, shoulders, arms, and legs, but still refused to let the American flag touch the ground. His loyalty was amazing since he was born a slave in Norfolk, VA, and escaped to the North. He joined the 54th Massachusetts Volunteer Infantry. Their assault at Fort Wagner was acted out in the 1989 movie, "Glory" that shows Carney getting shot multiple times, and as he handed the flag off to a fellow soldier after he crossed over into the Union side, he said, "Boys, I only did my duty; the old flag never touched the ground!" The flag to him represented the hopes he had for an America where all of the people have equal rights and equal opportunities. He joined the Union fighting for the freedom of all people.

2. One reason each regiment has a flag representing that regiment is so their location can be identified on the battlefield. The flag barriers were a target of the enemy, and many died trying to keep their regiment flag from being captured. At the Battle of Gettysburg in 1863, the 1st Massachusetts Infantry was retreating when **Nathaniel Allen** ran the opposite direction to rescue the flag. To save his

regiment from disgrace, he had to pull it out from under the body of the flag bearer in the middle of enemy fire and brought it back to his unit.

3. **Barbara Fritchie** refused to let the Confederates take down her flag. She displayed pride in her country when she scolded the men saying they could shoot every grey hair on her head but not the flag of their country. She didn't back down when they started to shoot at her, and she was willing to sacrifice her life to keep her flag waving.

4. On July 2nd, 1863, the **Minnesota 1st Volunteer Regiment** had been ordered to conduct a diversionary strike on the Confederates while the Union waited for reinforcements to show up at the three-day battle of Gettysburg. They were outnumbered but determined to hold the line until the reinforcements could arrive, and by that evening, the more than 250 brave sacrificial lambs had been reduced to 47 survivors. On July 3, 1863, **Private Marshall Sherman** of the Minnesota 1st found himself in the middle of the Union lines during the assault now known as "Pickett's Charge" ordered by Confederate General Robert E. Lee. Declared a Union victory, in the midst of the bloodiest battle of the Civil War, the barefoot and legendary Private Sherman captured the Virginian Battle Flag of the 28th Infantry. His valor earned him the Medal of Honor, and the flag remains "one of the true treasures of the Minnesota Historical Society," as stated on the Society's website. The amount of bloodshed for this flag is one reason that, despite requests and even a lawsuit to give the flag back to the state of Virginia, all requests were denied. President Grover Cleveland first issued an executive order in 1887 requesting the return of the colors of a few confederate units to show an act of good will. This order was challenged by men who fought on both sides including the former president of the Confederacy, Jefferson Davis, who, as reported in the Roanoke Times, said that banners belong to the captors by "all known military precedents."

President Cleveland rescinded the order, but the feud between Minnesota and Virginia over the flag continues to this day. It can be viewed in the Minnesota state capitol building.

5. On April 25, 1976, at a baseball game in Dodger Stadium, two people who happened to be Muslim were protestors who said they were going to burn our flag to show their support of ISIS. Right down in the outfield during a game, they poured gasoline on the flag and were ready to start it on fire when **Rick Monday** ran down and grabbed the flag and kept running bringing the flag to safety. Rick kept the flag and, although he was a great professional ball player, many joked that his "greatest play" was when he saved the American flag.

Our flag continues to be an inspirational symbol of the hopes and dreams we have for this land of the free and home of the brave. It may not be perfect yet, but when America's citizens unite, there are no limits to the greatness this country can achieve. May the flag continue to be an inspiring symbol that unites us all forevermore.

Both patriotism and the American flag have been the inspiration for music, artwork, books, movies, decorations, holidays, poems, jewelry, clothing, and, above all, it inspires us to feel and act patriotic! Here are a couple examples of amateur poetry that the author was inspired to write to show the author's patriotism.

Some of The American Auxiliary Post 311 Color Guard 2019, photo taken before the July 4th Parade.

The Flag a Symbol of Patriotism
By Tamara Thayer 2019

As I pledge allegiance to the flag of the United States of America, I put my right hand over my heart.
I pause to reflect what that allegiance really means and how we can prevent our country from falling apart.
There was special meaning for each color and shape as Betsy Ross sewed her masterpiece of pure art!
As we are reminded of all that the flag represents we see that there was so much thought put into each part

13 stars and stripes for the number of colonies that declared their independence making us free
One by one we added a sovereign state to the union and a new star too, until there's 50 stars I see
June 14, 1777, Congress declared the "national flag" for you and me.
May the pride Americans feel displaying them on "Flag Day" forever be!

The red stands for the blood shed by the brave who answered the call
To keep our freedoms............ all gave some and some gave all!
The white stands for faith and the right to worship without prosecution
We can pick our own religion to worship, or not, without persecution

The blue stands for life, justice and liberty, in each of our communities
The union represents equality and unity giving us all the same opportunities
Freedom of speech, religion, press, and the right to bear arms are just a few
of the ten amendments made in the Bill of Rights to keep freedoms for you
Look back at why we are the greatest country in the world and it's no mystery
Paul Revere, Patrick Henry, Barbara Fritchie, & Harriet Tubman in our history
Are ordinary people taking an extra ordinary stance in the midst of calamity
They inspire us to do all we can do to better our world for all of humanity

As we say the Pledge or sing the National Anthem, let's stand facing the flag with respect
When "for a cause" burning the flag or kneeling in protest often causes others to deject.
These actions only stir up anger and from the cause, no matter how good, others deflect
Instead show unity and stand up for the flag which represents all of our hopes as we reflect

Doing random acts of kindness and paying it forward should be the norm
A stronger unified country where neighbors help each other would soon form
Doing our part to make America revered again as the greatest country would be grand
Let's protect the environment so we can be proud to have our children inherit this land

Anyone or anything that would try to cause divide in this great country we need to reject
I will pledge allegiance to the flag and the foundations that this country was built on I will uphold and protect
Lincoln said, "A government of the people, for the people and by the people shall not perish."
I believe that the flag represents ALL of its people in the USA that I cherish!

The Veteran's Poppy

In Flanders Field the poppies grew
Their triumphant display of crimson red
Since WWI that poem we knew
Would honor veterans living and dead

Brave men and women have answered the call
To protect and serve the Red, White and Blue
All gave some and some gave all
How can we thank them, what should we do?

With the donations for the poppies you proudly wear
Which were made by our veterans, by the way
The auxiliary can support veterans to show we all care
With projects all year not just on Memorial Day

As the Legion family places flowers for the grave
of each fallen hero whose life was lost
May we never forget to honor the Brave
For our freedoms were not free but came at their cost!

Poppy Painting and Poem
By Tamara Louise Thayer
American Legion Auxiliary
Elysian, Minnesota Unit 311

Patriotism and the Flag have also Inspired Quotes:

"The Constitution was never meant to stop people from praying, Its declared purpose was to protect their rights to pray."
 -*Ronald Reagan*

"May we think of freedom not to do as we please, but as the opportunity to do what is right!"
 -*Peter Marshall*

"One flag, One land, One heart, One Nation, ever more".
 -*Oliver Wendall Holmes*

"Let every nation know, whether it wishes us well or ill, we shall pay any price, bear any burden, meet any hardship, support any friend, oppose any foe, to assure the success and survival of liberty."
 -*J.F. Kennedy*

"Sure I wave the American flag. Do you know a better flag to wave? Sure I love my country with all her faults. I'm not ashamed of that, never have been never will be."
 -*John Wayne*

"The time for war is done and now let us find peace."
戦争の時は終わりました。そして今、平和を見つけましょう。」
Sensō no toki wa owarimashita. Soshite ima, heiwa o mitsukemashou.'
 -*Dr. Ellsworth Thayer, captain in WWII serving as a doctor and surgeon on Tinian Island. After the atomic bombs were dropped and the Japanese Surrender, he was sent with his unit to Occupied Japan where he worked beside his new comrades, the Japanese doctors, to do aftercare in Fukuoka, Japan.*

"As Americans, we have the rights and freedoms to do anything as long as it doesn't infringe on the rights and freedoms of others. Don't take advantage of those freedoms and use them to tear down or disrespect what others have worked so hard to bring together in strength and unity!"
 -*Tamara Louise Thayer*

"In intertwining the history of the American flag, we unfold the story of America".
 -*Tamara Louise Thayer*

United States of America Flag
The Date the States Joined the Union and Other Flag Facts

"Within the flag's history we find the story of America!"
Tamara Thayer

Ratified the Constitution		#Stars	#	Date Flag Adopted	# of years Official
1. Delaware	December 7, 1787	13	1st	June 14, 1777	18 years
2. Pennsylvania	December 12, 1787	13		June 14, 1777	18 years
3. New Jersey	December 18, 1787	13		June 14, 1777	18 years
4. Georgia	January 2, 1788	13		June 14, 1777	18 years
5. Connecticut	January 9, 1788	13		June 14, 1777	18 years
6. Massachusetts	February 6, 1788	13		June 14, 1777	18 years
7. Maryland	April 28, 1788	13		June 14, 1777	18 years
8. South Carolina	May 23, 1788	13		June 14, 1777	18 years
9. New Hamphire	June 21, 1788	13		June 14, 1777	18 years
10. Virginia	June 25, 1788	13		June 14, 1777	18 years
11. New York	July 26, 1788	13		June 14, 1777	18 years
12. North Carolina	November 21, 1789	13		June 14, 1777	18 years
13. Rhode Island	May 19, 1790	13		June 14, 1777	18 years

Entered the Union

14. Vermont	March 4, 1791	14		June 14, 1777	18 years
15. Kentucky	June 1, 1792	15	2nd	May 1, 1795	23 years
16. Tennessee	June 1, 1796	15		May 1, 1795	23 years
17. Ohio	March 1, 1803	15		May 1, 1795	23 years
18. Louisiana	April 30, 1812	15		May 1, 1795	23 years
19. Indiana	December 11, 1816	15		May 1, 1795	23 years
20. Mississippi	December 10, 1817	20	3rd	Apr 13, 1818	1 year
21. Illinois	December 3, 1818	21	4th	July 4, 1819	1 year
22. Alabama	December 14, 1819	21		July 4, 1819	1 year
23. Maine	March 15, 1820	23	5th	July 4, 1820	2 years
24. Missouri	August 10, 1821	24	6th	July 4, 1822	14 years
25. Arkansas	June 15, 1836	25	7th	July 4, 1836	1 year
26 Michigan	January 26, 1837	26	8th	July 4, 1837	1 year
27. Florida	March 3, 1845	27	9th	July 4, 1845	1 year
28. Texas	December 29, 1845	28	10th	July 4, 1846	1 year
29. Iowa	December 28, 1846	29	11th	July 4, 1847	1 year
30. Wisconsin	May 29, 1848	30	12th	July 4, 1848	3 years
31. California	September 9, 1850	31	13th	July 4, 1851	7 years
32. Minnesota	May 11, 1858	32	14th	July 4, 1858	1 year
33 Oregon	February 14, 1859	33	15th	July 4, 1859	2 years
34. Kansas	January 29, 1861	34	16th	July 4, 1861	2 years
35 West Virginia	June 20, 1863	35	17th	July 4, 1863	2 years

36. Nevada	October 31, 1864	36	18th	July 4, 1865	2 years
37. Nebraska	March 1, 1867	37	19th	July 4, 1867	10 years
38 Colorado	August 1, 1876	38	20th	July 4, 1877	13 years
39. North Dakota	November 2, 1889	43	21st	July 4, 1890	1 year
40. South Dakota	November 2, 1889	43		July 4, 1890	1 year
41 Montana	November 8, 1889	43		July 4, 1890	1 year
42. Washington	November 11, 1889	43		July 4, 1890	1 year
43. Idaho	July 3, 1890	43		July 4, 1890	1 year
44. Wyoming	July 10, 1890	44	22nd	July 4, 1891	5 years
45. Utah	January 4, 1896	45	23rd	July 4, 1896	12 years
46. Oklahoma	November 16, 1907	46	24th	July 4, 1908	4 years
47. New Mexico	January 6, 1912	48	25th	July 4, 1912	47 years
48. Arizona	February 14, 1912	48		July 4, 1912	47 year
49. Alaska	January 3, 1959	49	26th	July 4, 1959	1 year
50. Hawaii	August 21, 1959	50	27th	July 4, 1960	current

History of the Flags Used on American Soil

Flags of the First Nations

In America, the First Nations didn't have flags for their bands before the colonies arrived; it was not part of their culture and was more of a European tradition. Since the 1990's when the federal government officially recognized the sovereign bands, they have been developing their own flags representing each tribe.

One of The Vikings Flags
came to The New World
c.1003 AD

Royal Standard of Spain
Columbus raised this
declaring the Americas for
Spain on October 12, 1492

151

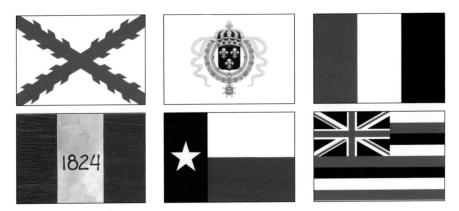

Spain, New France, France, Mexico,
The Republic of Texas, Hawaii, and England

Some of the *Early Flags used to* claim new territories in what is now The United States of America. Texas and Hawaii are the only two states to keep the original flag of their country before they became part of the United States of America.

"The Kings Colours" aka
"The Union Jack"

This British Flag was the flag of England from 1606 to 1801 and would have been the flag flown on American soil by the English Colonies sent to America under their rule.

Washington's Headquarters Flag

The Sons of Liberty 2nd Flag and The Boston Tea Party Flag

The first had just 9 stripes for the 9 colonies that signed the Stamp Act. The ships used this flag representing the 13 colonies.

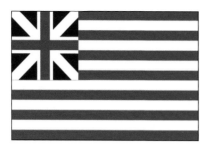

"The Continental Colors" aka "The Grand Union"

First American flag ordered by General George Washington at the Battle of Boston Jan. 2, 1776. The 13 stripes were added to represent the 13 colonies. Note: England in 1801 adopted a similar one to this with using stripes but added a layer of crosses to represent the new United Kingdom of Scotland, Ireland, and England. Each of their former flags had a cross so the new one layered them.

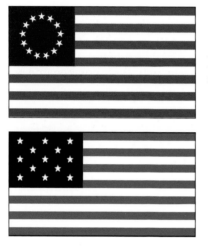

The Betsy Ross Flag

Designed by Betsy Ross and President George Washington.

The First "Official" United States Flag

On June 14th, 1777 this 13-Star flag became the Official United States flag and is the result of the congressional action that took place on that date. President George Washington (1789-1797) was the only president to serve under this flag. This flag continued for a period of 18 years.

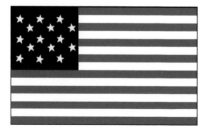

The Star Spangled Banner: 15 Stars and 15 Stripes

This was the flag for 23 years from May 1, 1795 to April 13, 1818. In September, 1814, the British Navy attacked Baltimore Harbor's Fort McHenry, and this is the flag that Francis Scott Key hoped was still waving after the British attack. He later wrote a poem about that night, and it became our official Star Spangled Banner song.

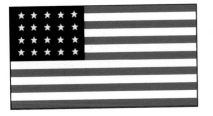

"Old Glory"

This 20 stars and 13 stripes flag was our third official flag on April 13, 1818, and it is the style Sea Captain William Driver flew over his ship. He had a handmade one given as a gift from his mom and other women that he treasured. He was the first to nickname it "Old Glory!" Later during the Civil War when the Confederates tried on more than one occasion to seize his flag, he famously protected his revered flag by saying, "If you want my flag, you'll have to take it over my dead body!" He later sewed it into a coverlet to hide it until after the war. It is on display at the Smithsonian Institution in the National Museum of American History.

The Barbara Fritchie Flag

The 34-Star Flag: On July 4th, 1861, this flag became the Official United States flag. The 34th state was Kansas added on January 29th, 1861 and this flag of 34 stars continued for two years. The only president to serve under this flag was Abraham Lincoln (1861-1865). This is the flag Barbara Fritchie waved at Stonewall Jackson's men. During the Civil War, many versions of this flag were seen as there was not any official pattern for how the 34 stars should be placed on the blue union of the flag, and during the four year war, the number of stars started at 33, 34, 35 and there were 36 stars by the end of the war in 1865. Many creative patterns of how to display these stars were created.

**First of 3 official CSA flags
7, 9, and 12 stars**

This flag during the Civil War belonged to a Mississippi Regiment on display in Minnesota.

**The Confederate Battle Flag
Most commonly used
by the CSA**

This 12 star flag represented the 12 states that seceded from the Union and went to war during the "Great War of the Rebellion" or The "Civil War" to create the Confederate States of America (CSA).

This is the **3rd official CSA flag** with 13 stars representing the 11 states that seceded and Kentucky and Missouri. The 2nd official one did not have the red stripe on the end, but otherwise was identical.

Minnesota 7th Regiment Flag
(The battles they fought in are written on the flag)

Minnesota 7th Regiment Flag

Civil War Regimental Flags
Both the Union and Confederate regiments had their own battle flags.

The Iwo Jima Flag

The 48 Star Flag: On July 4,1912, the U.S. flag grew to 48 stars with the addition of New Mexico (January 6, 1912) and Arizona (February 14, 1912). In the Executive Order of President Taft dated June 24, 1912, the proportions of the flag and the star pattern were defined officially. It provided for arrangement of the stars in six horizontal rows of eight each, a single point of each star to be upward. This flag was official for 47 years through World War I, II, and the Korean War. The famous raising of the American flag after the battle of Iwo Jima was this 48 star flag. Eight presidents served under this flag; William Taft, Woodrow Wilson, Warren Harding, Calvin Coolidge, Herbert Hoover, Franklin Roosevelt, Harry S. Truman, and Dwight D. Eisenhower.

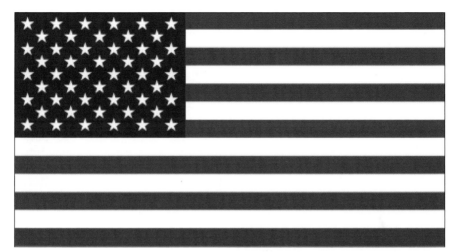

The Flag of the
United States of America

The 50 Star Flag: Adopted on July 4, 1960, after the 50th state of Hawaii was added on August 21, 1959. This became the 27th official flag of the United States. July 4, 2020 is the 60th anniversary of this flag. This is the flag style; on the moon, raised at Ground Zero on 9-11-01, and proudly displayed today by the American people.

TIMELINE

Putting the events that affected Barbara, her family, friends, and community in order to get a better perspective of it all:

1755 A young George Washington was visiting in Frederick, Maryland, when he met General Braddick who was there waiting for new supplies to arrive. General Braddick asked Washington to be his Aide-de-Camp, and he accepted.

October 1756 Colonel George Washington started making a personal survey of the frontier between Maryland and North Carolina. The purpose was to build a chain of forts to protect the colonists. One of the sturdiest of these ramparts was Fort Frederick, in Frederick, Maryland. He continued to make several trips to Frederick.

December 3, 1766 Barbara Fritchie was born in Lancaster, PA.

December 16, 1766 Barbara was baptized by Rev. Hendal in Lancaster.

1776 Barbara's family moved from Lancaster to Frederick, MD, when she was ten years old.

1777 Thomas Johnson from Frederick, MD was Maryland's first elected governor. He nominated his personal friend George Washington for his post of Commander and Chief of the Continental Army.

1786 Barbara showed an interest in politics and waited on General George Washington serving tea on his many trips to Frederick.

Comparing census reports:

1790 census	shows John Fritchie living in Frederick and both a Nicolas and Daniel "Hower" instead of Hauer
1800 & 1810 census	no Fritchie or Hauers, Where was Barbara during this time"?"
1820 census	there is John Fritchie listed, four Hauer households; Daniel Sr, Daniel Jr, Elizabeth M., George
1830 census	John C Fritchie, four Hauer households; Daniel Sr, Elizabeth, Henry, George

John C Fritchie and Francis Scott Key were the same age from Frederick, Maryland. Barbara was friends with both of them.

June 30, 1791	George Washington made his first official visit into Frederick as "President" of the United States and had a formal banquet at Kimball's Tavern.
1797-1806	The Kimball Tavern and Inn was located on part of the site where the current Francis Scott Key Hotel was built.
December 14, 1799	George Washington died. Barbara and Francis Scott Key planned his public memorial in Frederick. Barbara was 33 years old.

Birth of a daughter named Barbara, date unknown

May 6, 1806	Marriage to John Casper Fritchie when Barbara was 39 years old.

Barbara and John remained friends with Francis Scott Key.

September 14, 1814　Fort McHenry was attacked and Francis Scott

Key wrote a poem about his experience originally called "The Defense of Fort M'Henry." This later became known as the official national anthem, The Star-Spangled Banner.

About 1850	Mary Colburn was born in either Oneida, NY, or Corning, NY (she was Barbara's granddaughter).
November 10, 1849	John Fritchie died; he was buried in the German Reformed graveyard.
February 4, 1860	The states that wanted to secede from the Union sent delegates to meet in Montgomery, Alabama to form their new provisional government.
November 6, 1860	Abraham Lincoln was elected president of the United States.
December 20, 1860	South Carolina was the first state to secede from the Union.
February 9, 1861	Jefferson Davis from Mississippi was elected the president of the Confederate States of America.
March 4, 1861	Abraham Lincoln, the 16th president of the United States of America, was inaugurated. Administering the oath of office was Chief Justice Roger Brooke Taney. Taney was a local from Frederick, Maryland.
April 12 – 13, 1861	Confederate troops attacked the Union at Fort Sumter which starts the Civil War.

Minnesota's Governor Alexander Ramsey happened to be in the Washington DC meeting with President Lincoln when word of Fort

Sumter came. Minnesota made history when it became the first state to offer men to fight for the Union cause in the Civil War following Lincoln's request. The governor offered the US Secretary of War 1,000 Minnesota soldiers on that day, and, by the end of the war, about 25,000 soldiers from Minnesota had fought in 21 different units.

July 21, 1861   The First Battle of Manassas called the Battle of Bull Run took place in Virginia. Colonel Thomas Jackson's bravery during battle earned him the nickname "Stonewall Jackson".

March 9, 1862   The first battle between ironclad warships the USS Monitor and the CSS Virginia.

April 6 -7, 1862   Union victory at the Battle of Shiloh left more than 23,000 men killed in action. Shiloh Battlefield is in Tennessee about 787 miles from Frederick, MD. In just five months, the war was just outside of Frederick.

August 29 – 30, 1862   The Second Battle of Manassas was fought, resulting in a Confederate victory. Manassas is 59.7 miles from Frederick, MD.

September 5, 1862   Generals Longstreet and Stonewall Jackson's troops set up camp 2 1/2 miles outside of Frederick preparing for their next battle.

5:00am on September 6, 1862

    Stonewall and a small group of men came to Frederick for supplies. Stonewall supposedly left a note on Dr. Ross's door near the home of Barbara. Dr. Ross was a Presbyterian Pastor and friend of Stonewall Jackson. (This note went missing and later one dated Sept. 10th surfaced).

September 6, 1862   Barbara Fritchie's famous flag waving to the confederate troops took place.

September 7, 1862   General Stonewall Jackson attended the German Reformed Church service in the evening. He was witnessed to have fallen asleep during the service while sitting toward the back of the church. Dr. Zacharias prayed for the President of the United States, but he slept through it.

September 10, 1862   The Confederate Army marched through Frederick, MD, down Patrick Street. Mary Quantrill's flag waving supposedly took place.

September 12, 1862   The Union Army marched through Frederick passing in front of Barbara's house. Some sources say that General Jesse Reno had already heard about Barbara's flag incident and had stopped at her home to hear it from her directly. Barbara offered him tea and baked goodies while she told him of her ordeal. She served him some of her homemade wine, and he asked to use her writing table to write a letter home. He asked for the large flag used in the incident, but Barbara not wanting to give it up, gave her smaller silk flag to General Reno.

September 16, 1862   In the Battle of South Mountain, General Reno was killed and Barbara's flag was found underneath his coat. It was sent back with his body to his family in Massachusetts.

September 16 – 18, 1862

   The Army of the Potomac attacked Robert E. Lee's forces in Maryland at the Battle of

Antietam, which was the bloodiest battle of the Civil War. After the Union victory, the Confederates retreated from Maryland.

December 3, 1862   Barbara turned 96 and had a large birthday party to celebrate with her family and friends.

Barbara became ill following her birthday party. She died just 15 days later from pneumonia. Many sources state that she was very healthy and active right up to catching the pneumonia.

December 18, 1862   Barbara died and was buried in her church cemetery next to her husband John. Several of her relatives are also buried in the same church cemetery. Her house was left to her niece Catherine Hanshaw who lived there until 1866.

January 1, 1863   President Lincoln delivered the Emancipation Proclamation which only set the slaves in the Confederate states free. This did not apply to the border states who had slavery but were part of the Union during the Civil War. It took almost two years later with a new Constitution before Maryland would free their slaves on November 1, 1864.

March 3, 1863   Congress passed the conscription act which stated all men between the ages of 20 and 45 must register to serve in the military.

July 1 – 3, 1863   The Battle of Gettysburg.

1863   John Greenleaf Whittier heard about Barbara Fritchie's flag waving from several people as well as read about it in many newspapers. He wrote the poem Barbara Frietchie in the summer.

October 1863	Whittier's poem was published in the Atlantic magazine.
November 19, 1863	President Lincoln delivered the Gettysburg Address.
1864	Albert Augustus Thayer served in Company C of the Minnesota 7th Volunteer Regiment as a drummer boy.
1864	William Cooper of the Minnesota 8th Regiment, company B, was wounded in the Battle of the Cedars in Murfreesburough, Tennessee. He survived the war and later one of his 3 daughters, Maude, married David LeRoy Thayer the great grandson of Barbara Fritchie.
November 1, 1864	Under a new U.S. Constitution, the border states that formerly had been allowed to maintain their slavery during the Civil War, freed them. Jacob Engelbrecht summed it up best in his diary: "Free Maryland - from this day forward and forever the state of Maryland is free from it's foul blot of slavery - until yesterday, there were more than ninety-thousand slaves in Maryland, (and about eighty thousand free blacks) 'all men are created free.'"
January 31, 1865	Congress abolished slavery.
April 9, 1865	Robert E. Lee surrendered the Army of Northern Virginia which ended the war.
April 14, 1865	President Lincoln was assassinated.
1866	Catherine Hanshaw sold her house (formerly Barbara Fritchie's house) to George Eissler. Tourists flocked to see the house.

1868   The Caroll Creek rose above its banks damaging the baseboards of the Barbara Fritchie house.

1868/1869   The town of Frederick wanted to widen the Creek to prevent future flooding so they condemned Barbara's house rather than restore it. At this time, the wood from her window frame was made into walking canes and sold. Whittier and General Cox each had one.

1868   After the house was taken down, tourists continued to ask where her house was and so a sign marking the original location was put up. Her story spread, and soon she was an international household name. School children recited her poem.

July 5, 1869   Mary A Colburn and Albert Augustus Thayer were married in Hennepin County, Minnesota. Mary was Barbara's granddaughter.

December 24, 1871   Mary and Albert Thayer welcomed the birth of their first son, William Warren Thayer, in Osseo, Minnesota. William was the great grandson of Barbara Fritchie.

November 4, 1873   Mary and Albert Thayer celebrated the birth of their second son, David LeRoy Thayer in Osseo, Minnesota. David lost his mother when he was just two months old.

January 11, 1874   Mary A. (Colburn) Thayer died at the age of 23, just a couple months after giving birth to her second son, David LeRoy Thayer.

August 7, 1879   Mary Quantrill's obituary appeared in the Frederick newspaper on this date. The wording of the obituary was one last attempt to make a mockery of the fame of the real Barbara Fritchie.

1893   The Confederate Veteran newspaper wrote a very sarcastic spoof on Barbara Fritchie, mocking her and, unfortunately, people took it seriously adding to the misinformation about her. This source said she was sick in bed, among many false statements.

1913   The Barbara Fritchie Memorial Association was formed. They started plans to have both Barbara and John moved from the Reformed Church graveyard to Mount Olivet Cemetery. They began plans to honor Barbara's memory with a monument. The Association also sparked a renewed interest in the flag and patriotism as well as promoted the heroism and bravery of Barbara.

May 30, 1914   Reinterment of Barbara and John Fritchie in the Mt. Olivet Cemetery. Her casket was opened at Mt. Olivet Cemetery and some of her personal items with which she was buried were removed and displayed in the museum.

September 9, 1914   The new Barbara Fritchie Monument was revealed at her gravesite, and it was dedicated during the Centennial Celebration of the Star-Spangled Banner.

Note: The Barbara Fritchie Monument, dedicated in 1914, is 13 feet tall and is made of Maryland Guilford Granite. The monument contains the bronze seal of the Barbara Fritchie Memorial Association over a bronze plaque bearing the poem, "Barbara Freitchie" written by John Greenleaf Whittier.

1915 and 1924   Two silent movie versions were released about Barbara Fritchie. The first one came out in 1915, and the second one came out in 1924. Very little follows the true story of Barbara the subject of this book, and more of the silent movie follows the love story of the grandparents of the movie director.

1918   The Barbara Fritchie Restaurant opened in Frederick. They sold some memorabilia and Barbara Fritchie candies at this restaurant.

1926   The Barbara Fritchie house was rebuilt at only 2/3 scale and moved farther away from Caroll Creek. The museum housed her original artifacts such as a shawl Francis Scott Key gave her, the coffee pot she used to serve guests like George Washington, and the tea set he gave her as a gift, dainty cookie cutters, the bed in which she died, her writing desk, original chairs, etc.

July 4, 1927   The Barbara Fritchie house was dedicated with all pomp and circumstance with a large crowd and dignitaries from Maryland and Massachusetts. The house has been a major tourist attraction ever since.

March 3, 1931   The Star Spangled Banner became the official national anthem of the United States as President Herbert Hoover signed a congressional resolution.

1937   Henry Ford commissioned a replica of five historic homes as part of this Colonial Village at Dearborn Inn, Dearborn, Michigan. They are the 5 homes of Barbara Fritchie, Edgar Allen Poe, Walt Whitman, Oliver Wolcott, and Patrick Henry. These homes are replicas - exact duplicates.

1943   Winston Churchill was with the US President Franklin D. Roosevelt on their way to Shangra-la (now called Camp David), and he asked to stop by her house. Winston stopped and recited her entire poem from memory.

After WWII, Dwight D. Eisenhower, bought a home near Gettysburg which is close to Frederick. He visited Frederick and its historic landmarks including the Barbara Fritchie House. He bought one of her souvenir walking sticks made of the wood from her window frame in her original house.

1944   Dr. William Quynn wrote a 45-page book stating that he didn't think his great great aunt did the flag waving. He spoke in a very negative manner of her in his book. His father was D. Hauer Quynn who was the one family member from Barbara's side who had joined the group debunking her story. The other family member of Barbara was from her husband's side of the family.

April 15, 1955   In The Frederick Post, Frederick, Maryland, in the article "So They Tell Me" by Betty Sullivan, she recapped a clipping from the Chicago Record from December 12, 1897, about two brothers who claim to be descendants of Barbara Fritchie's sister. The two brothers, J. L. Wheeler, the Justice of Peace at Deer Park, and H. H. Wheeler of Roulesburg, West Virginia, claimed Barbara Fritchie as a sister of their paternal grandmother. They said Barbara Fritchie's father was John Fritchie. Could they be talking about the "daughter" Barbara Fritchie to whom the author has made reference in this book? Some of their facts do not line up, however, with the way history has recorded the story of Casper Fritchie being hanged for treason.

1963 In the fifth TV season of Rocky and Bullwinkle, a spoof was made of the Barbara Fritchie poem with Bullwinkle playing the part of Barbara.

1986 Barbara Fritchie artifacts were donated to the Evangelical Reformed Church by Mrs. Cornelia Rodock who had obtained them from her cousin, Miss Eleanor Abbott, who initially inherited them from her mother, Julia Hanshaw Abbott.

2018 The Barbara Fritchie Restaurant in Frederick closed after 100 years in business.

2019 Bryan and Charlotte Chaney renovated the former Barbara Fritchie replica home, formerly used as a museum and turned it into a beautiful place to stay while in Frederick now known as The Barbara Fritchie AirBnB. This was walking distance to most of the tourist attractions around town. They did an excellent job of preserving her history while incorporating updated conveniences of modern living.

BARBARA (HAUER) FRITCHIE'S DESCENDANTS

The Thayer family oral history passed down for generations states that they descended from the famous Barbara Fritchie. This book is the story of the author's fourth great-grandmother as first told to her through these generations of oral and written history and then confirmed through her years of research.

Barbara (Hauer) Fritchie (1766 - 1862)
fourth great-grandmother

Barbara Fritchie
Daughter of Barbara (Hauer) Fritchie

Mary A. Colburn (1850 - 1874)
Daughter of Barbara (Fritchie) and Daniel Colburn

LeRoy David "Roy" Thayer (1873 - 1930)
Son of Mary A. (Colburn) and Albert Augustus Thayer

Dr. Ellsworth Albert Thayer (1907 - 2000)
Son of LeRoy David "Roy" Thayer and Maude Allana (Cooper)

David Leroy Thayer (1931 - 2014)
Son of Dr. Ellsworth Albert Thayer and Helen Kathyrn (Gallehue)

Tamara Louise Thayer
Daughter of David Leroy Thayer and Edna Louise (Wilke)

Note: For anyone wanting to research and verify that this information on each of these generations is correct, some information is clarified. Barbara's great grandson was given the name of David LeRoy Thayer at birth but, after he married, he changed his name to LeRoy David

Thayer and often went by "Roy" Thayer. For a lot of records on Albert Augustus Thayer, he went by A. A. Thayer or "Gus". Annandale Advocate newspaper articles talking about "Albert" Thayer were usually talking about his 3rd son, Albert Thayer who later commonly went by "Bert". When Helen Gallehue was born, her middle name was spelled "Kathryn", but after she graduated with her RN degree she cleverly changed her middle name to Kathyrn to resemble "Kathy + RN". David Leroy Thayer didn't capitalize the "r" in Leroy like his grandfather. These simple name changes do not seem like a big deal but, as genealogists know, it makes it hard to match up the right records with people when there has been a name change. For example, there is a national Thayer Families Association that has thoroughly researched and maintained records of the surname Thayer in America going back to their arrival in the 1630's and following their descendants to the current generations. David LeRoy Thayer was on their online list of "displaced Thayers" because, after finding a birth record for him, there wasn't a marriage or death record of the same name.

Barbara Fritchie is the daughter of Barbara (Hauer) Fritchie. She married Daniel Colburn. It is unknown if Daniel and Barbara Fritchie Colburn had other children besides Mary Colburn. One source says there was also a son named Will Colburn. Pictures of the daughter Barbara Fritchie, and one of her granddaughter Mary Colburn are found earlier in this book.

Albert "Gus" Thayer   *The Thayer Hotel, Annandale, Minnesota*

Albert Thayer was just 15 years old when he was a drummer boy for the Minnesota 7th Regiment, Company C. Barbara's granddaughter, Mary Colburn married Albert Augustus Thayer in Annandale, Minnesota, following the Civil War. Albert was in the service with his friend Henry Curtis from Annandale. After the Civil War was over, Henry was a witness in Albert and Mary's wedding. The other witness was Albert's sister Francis Thayer. Two months later, Henry Curtis married Albert's sister, Francis Thayer and Albert and Mary were witnesses to their wedding. Albert and Mary had two children: William Warren Thayer and David LeRoy Thayer. Perhaps Mary had complications with her delivery which was common during this time period because she died just a couple months later after having her son David at the age of 24. Albert's life is summed up best in this creative poem:

The Spirit of Adventurous Albert Augustus (Gus) Thayer
Written by Edna Louise Thayer

September, 2019

The spirit of Albert Augustus is alive and well
In the haunted house of the Thayer Hotel.
Albert was born in Adrian, Michigan, December 28th, 1948,
A Christmas gift to David Burgess and Catherine Warren — a few days late.
For those of you who follow ancestry —
This line of Thayers is from the Thomas Thayer tree.
Albert Augustus, whose nickname was Gus,
Was filled with spirit and adventurous.
He came to MN with his parents at the age of five—
Homesteading a farm near Osseo was an adventure to stay alive,
They cleared the land, built a log house with dirt floors & led a pioneer life.
Harsh weather, grasshoppers, and drought caused some fear and strife.
They kept the horses harnessed day and night —
So they could flee at first sign of Indian fright.

Gus lied about his age when he was still 15.

Enlisting as a drummer boy for the Union he was seen.

He served with the MN 7th Volunteer Infantry Regiment, Company C.

After he fought in one of the last Civil War battles in Alabama at Fort Blakely—

He was hospitalized in Montgomery prior to his discharge upon returning.

Many soldiers suffered from diseases such as scurvy and food poisoning.

His father died in 1873, eight years after the war.

And Gus operated the farm until 1878, five years more.

April, 1869, Gus married Mary Colburn, the granddaughter of Barbara Fritchie.

As Stonewall Jackson passed her house, Barbara waved her Union flag with glee.

Her patriotism was immortalized in a John Greenleaf Whittier poem—

Mary's family was spirited as well; her mother was disowned when she left home-

To go with a coachman to the Oneida Community in New York.

This was a commune better known for making knives, spoons, and forks.

When the commune closed, Mary traveled with a small group to relocate.

They came to MN and lived on a farm near Gus. Mary meeting Gus was fate.

After Mary gave birth to two sons, William Warren & David Leroy, alive,

Mary died two months after childbirth in 1875.

In 1980, Gus married Carrie J. Hill, and then—

With another five children, God blessed them.

To have just one job, Gus was never content.

It required multiple, simultaneous adventures before his energy was spent.

When he farmed after the army, he bought one of the first threshing machines,

And did custom work for neighbors to supplement his means.

He had a Star mail route between St. Cloud and Fair Haven.

His friendly operating of a stage coach over this route kept customers "ravin'".

After the hotel fire in 1894, he was appointed constable of Annandale.

For this job, his negotiating and compromising skills made him very able.

Gus was probably best known for his hotel management.

He managed the Star Hotel in Fair Haven, before he went—

To Annandale in 1889 to manage the Annandale House,

Which he did very effectively with his spouse.

In 1894, the "House" caught fire and burned down.

Leaving many of the city residents with a frown.
The Soo Line Railroad was most upset
To lose the Hotel which had become a great asset.
They donated the land so Gus could rebuild,
The city helped with labor and furnishings, it's been told.
The hotel was a first to have electricity and gas lights.
Events and parties became a delight.
Gus would play the piano and entertain,
While Carrie's reputation for excellent food gained in fame.
Generous Gus often would bring friends home to eat;
Typically he didn't charge — it was his treat.
The city paid them a little to feed destitute men,
The cooking and work was done by Caroline for them.
The hotel hosting of many of the city's special events were a delight,
As well as meetings i.e. the G.A.R. (Grand Army of the Republic) on a given night.
His obituary described Gus as active, energetic, an honorable gentleman and more,
Who gave liberally of his time and talents, He died March 1923, at age 74
It further stated, "He extended a cordial greeting that bent a ray of light—
To others so their pathway in the journey of life was bright."

Gus still walks the halls of the Thayer Hotel today.
It's listed as one of the top 10 best haunted places to stay in the USA.
Guests report lights go off and on, plus creaking and groaning noises at night;
Propped open doors will close, the ghosts are friendly and don't cause a fright.
Some see the rocking of Gus's granddaughter, Blanche's chair.
And the smell of Gus's cigar and ghost kittens will appear.
It feels like Gus and Caroline are very near,
the piano playing the same piece over and over again some can hear
The hotel was placed on the National Historic Site Register in 1978.
One can feel the presence of Gus and Caroline at work to keep it great.

Albert was very active in getting a reunion or small gathering together of Civil War veterans and hosted them at the Thayer Hotel.

He would play the piano and they would sing their former Civil War songs and tell stories of their time served. Mary would have been a part of hosting these early veteran reunions and get-to-gethers. Mary passed away in 1879 and is buried in the Brooklyn and Maple Grove Union Cemetery in Maple Grove, Minnesota. Later in 1883 Albert was an integral part in starting the GAR unit in his town of Annandale, Minnesota.

Mary A. (Colburn) Thayer, wife of Albert and granddaughter of Barbara (Hauer) Fritchie is buried in Annandale, Minnesota, next to her in-laws, David Burgess Thayer and Catherine Warren Thayer. Catherine helped take care of her grandsons William and David until their father Albert Thayer married Caroline Hill. Albert and Caroline then had five more children. The family owned the Thayer Hotel, and all seven of their children grew up in Annandale.

Of Albert's seven children, only the descendants of **Willam Warren Thayer** and **LeRoy David Thayer** are descendants of the Barbara (Hauer) Fritchie from Frederick, Maryland. A summary of these two remarkable men and a brief explanation of the next generation of descendants follows:

The following article about **William Warren Thayer** is from "History of Lincoln, Oneida and Vilas Counties, Wisconsin" compiled by George O. Jones, Norman S. McVean and others. Published 1924 by H. C. Cooper, Jr. & Co. Since it was printed in 1924, the former abbreviations used for states and old fashion language were left to transcribe this article exactly as is. Also, Fair Haven was originally spelled as two words, and later this township changed its spelling to Fairhaven. It is correct in this book and not a typo. The article did not have anything in bold, but the author chose to put just the part about Barbara Fritchie in bold for emphasis:

"William W. Thayer, whose operations in land have given Oneida County many new farms and increased her rural population, was born at Osseo, Minn., Dec. 24, 1871, son of Albert A. and Mary (Colburn) Thayer. **The mother is said to have been a direct descendant (in which case probably a granddaughter) of the Barbara Freitchie of Frederick Town, Md., who in Civil War days, according to Whittier's poem, showed her patriotic union sentiments by braving Stonewall Jackson when he ordered his troops to shoot down a United States flag in front of her house ...**

When this wonderful article about William was printed in 1929, who would have known that he would die just 3 years later in an awful accident? William's obituary in this book, included previously, also states in it that he is the great grandson of Barbara Fritchie.

Mable and William Warren Thayer William is the great grandson of Barbara (Hauer) Fritchie

Front Row: Mary Elizabeth Thayer (she went by her middle name Elizabeth), sitting on his mom's lap is the future Dr. Ellsworth Albert Thayer. In the middle is Maude Allana (Cooper) Thayer, wife of LeRoy. Back row: William Cooper Thayer, and LeRoy David Thayer.

Elizabeth Thayer (in bottom left corner of picture) married Ben Ohslund, and they had one daughter, named Barbara Ohslund after the famous patriot Barbara Fritchie. Barbara married Curt Tasa, and they had 3 children: Jim, Robert, and Becky.

The author of this book is the granddaughter of Dr. Ellsworth Albert Thayer (sitting on his mother's lap in the photo). Dr. Thayer named his first son David Leroy after his father who had just passed away the year before. David Leroy married Edna Louise (Wilke) Thayer, and they are the parents of Scott, Tamara, and Brenda. Dr. Thayer's second son is William Roger Thayer who married Elaine (Williams) Thayer, and they had three children: Allen, Roger, and Dr. Kimberly Thayer. Dr. Thayer's daughter is Suzanne Alana (Thayer) Wright who first married Al Bakken, and they are the parents of Steve Bakken. She then married William Wright, and their children are Jenny, Joni, and Doug. One can read about the fascinating life of Dr. Ellsworth Albert Thayer in the book, *A Country Doctor Goes To War*.

William Cooper Thayer (standing in the second row on left side of the picture), married Claire Radik and had no children. His second wife was Claudia Swenson, and they had one daughter, Rosemary Lee (Thayer) Hortin.

Maude Allana (Cooper) Thayer (sitting in the middle of the family photo) is the daughter of Lizzie (Noyes) and William Cooper. She is the wife of LeRoy.

LeRoy (standing in the back row on the right), was from Osseo, MN when he married Maude from Fair Haven, MN. They lived in Annandale and Monticello for a few years each while he was a banker. He moved the family to Kensal, ND to start his own bank. After a couple years, he sold his bank, moving his family to Clarissa, Minnesota, where he started a new bank. He invested in farms. He lost everything in the Great Depression: his banks, three farms, stocks, and his house. He moved to Minneapolis for the last seven years of his life working as a teller in a bank and a second job in a grocery store. He died at 56 from a heart attack.

GLOSSARY

Abolish - to formally put an end to (a system, practice, or institution).

Abolitionist - a person who favors the abolishment of a practice or institution, especially capital punishment or (formerly) slavery.

Aide-de-Camp or Aide D'Camp - a military officer acting as a confidential assistant to a senior officer.

Artillery - 1. large-caliber guns used in warfare on land. 2. a military detachment or branch of the armed forces that uses large-caliber guns.

Battalion - a large body of troops ready for battle, especially an infantry unit forming part of a brigade typically commanded by a lieutenant colonel.

Battery - a fortified emplacement for heavy guns.
i.e. an artillery subunit of guns, men, and vehicles.
Brevet- when a commissioned officer is promoted in rank and title because of outstanding service, or as an award for gallantry or meritorious service, but is not given the increase in pay.

Brigade - a subdivision of an army, typically consisting of a small number of infantry battalions and/or other units and forming part of a division.

Bushwacker - in Missouri and other Border States of the Western Theater, guerilla fighters— were commonly called "bushwackers," although pro-Union partisans were also known as "jayhawkers," a term that had originated during the pre-war Bleeding Kansas period.
Carte - a card, playing card, chart, map, menu. Many of the early photographs were done on a thicker card stock.

Cartridge - a casing containing a charge and a bullet or shot for small arms or an explosive charge for blasting.

Casualty - 1. a person killed or injured in a war or accident.
2. a person or thing badly affected by an event or situation.

Cavalry - 1. (in the past) soldiers who fought on horseback. 2. modern soldiers who fight in armored vehicles.

Company - a military unit, typically consisting of 80–150 soldiers and usually commanded by a major or a captain. Most companies are formed of three to six platoons, although the exact number may vary by country, unit type, and structure.

Confederate - the Confederate States Army (C.S.A.) was the military land force of the Confederate States of America known as the Confederacy that fought against the United States forces during the American Civil War 1861 – 1865.

Confederacy - also known at the "Confederate States of America", or as "the South" or "the Confederacy" during the American Civil War it consisted officially of 11 southern slave states and from their point of view they add two of the border states to a total of 13 states and one western territory.

Conscript - also called the draft, conscription legally requires people to join the army, with penalties if they don't.

Draft - compulsory recruitment for military service.

Emigrant vs. immigrant vs. migrant - Emigrate means to leave one's country to live in another. Immigrate is to come into another country to live permanently. Migrate is to move for part of the year, living in one area and then moving back again to the original area to live for the rest of the year.

Emancipation - 1. to be set free from slavery. 2. the process of being set free from legal, social, and political injustices 3. Emancipation of minors is a legal process by which a minor, underaged child, is freed from control by their parents or guardians, and the parents or guardians are freed from any and all responsibility toward the child.
Emolument - for profit or salary or fee from employment.

Enlist - to enroll in the armed services.

Foundry - a workshop or factory for casting metal.

Johann Nicklaus Hauer - was born in Germany In 1733. He immigrated to Philadelphia, Pennsylvania in 1754 and started working there as a hat maker. He was the father of Barbara (Hauer) Fritchie.

Infantry - soldiers fighting on foot.

Manumissions - the process to free a slave, which the definition changes as the laws changed in America. In 1691 in Virginia, freeing a slave by will or deed was legal. In 1723 in Virginia that became illegal and a slave could only earn manumissions from some meritorious service and must be approved by the governor which reportedly seldom was granted. The Manumission laws in Maryland and Virginia were rewritten after the Revolutionary War.

Metanoia - 1. A transformational change in ones way of life.
2. A change resulting from repentance and spiritual awareness.

Militia - is an army or some other fighting organization or group of non-professional or non-trained soldiers. Militia can be called upon for military service during a time of need.

Oneida Community - a perfectionist religious communal society located in Oneida, New York, that was founded in 1848 by John Humphrey Noyes.

Pacifist - a person who refuses to be drafted or join in military activities because of their beliefs.[19]

---

[19] Author's personal definition of a pacifist is the following. Most people believe that violence is wrong and strive for peace. When other countries threaten that security, our country must try negotiations and compromises as they talk out their differences. If that is unsuccessful, then brave military will defend and fight to keep our freedoms. If more help is needed, we will draft, or civilians will form volunteer militia to defend their country. Pacifists will not fight for any reason. No matter how much their country needs them, they will refuse to join the military and if drafted they will flee the country until the war is over. Pacifists will wait for the brave to win the war and return to their country once there is peace again. Synonyms are draft dodgers, military protesters, conscientious objectors.

Patriot - a person who loves, supports, and defends his or her country and its interests with devotion, even willing to sacrifice ones own life to do so. The determining factor of whether or not one is considered a patriot or a rebel, rests solely on the outcome of the conflict.

Pioneer - is one of the first settlers in a new place.

Quartermaster - is a soldier whose job is to hand out supplies like food and clothes.

Rebel - n. a person who takes part in an armed rebellion against the constituted authority (especially in the hope of improving conditions) v. to take part in a rebellion; renounce a former allegiance. The determining factor of whether or not one is considered a patriot or a rebel, rests solely on the outcome of the conflict.

Recruit - v. to convince someone to join something. To enlist someone in the armed forces. "Lee tried to recruit soldiers from Frederick, Maryland." n. a person newly enlisted in the armed forces and not yet fully trained.

Regiment - army unit smaller than a division.

Regular Army - the official armed forces of a state or country, contrasting with irregular forces, such as volunteer irregular militias, private armies, mercenaries, etc. A standing army is the permanent force of the regular army that is maintained under arms during peacetime.

Secede - to withdraw formally from an alliance or association. "There were 10 Southern states in America that wanted to secede from the Union and form the Confederate States of America."

Shrapnel - 1. shell containing lead pellets that explodes in flight 2. fragments from an exploding bomb, mine, or shell

Volunteer - A military volunteer is a person who enlists in military service by free will, and is not a conscript, mercenary, or a foreign legionnaire. Troops raised as state militia were always described as "volunteers", even when recruited by conscription.

Skirmish - a minor battle

Soul Driver - starting in about the late 1600's and continuing until the Emancipation Proclamation in America, Soul Drivers were men who would board a new ship arriving in America that was carrying indentured servants or convicts and sell them into slavery for the profit and benefit of the Soul Driver. These servants and convicts were white, Native American, black, Asian, etc.

Tack - hard tack, a type of biscuit made from unleavened flour, water, and sometimes salt, was commonly used to stave off hunger on both sides.

Tactic - The art of disposing armed forces in order of battle and of organizing operations, especially during contact with an enemy.

Union - During the American Civil War, the North was also known at the Union. The Union was the United States of America and the national government of President Abraham Lincoln and the 20 free states, and 4 border states with slaves and some with split governments and troops sent both North and South.

Vexillology - is the study of the history, symbolism and usage of flags. To have an interest in flags.

Vexillologist - A person who studies flags.

Vexillographer - A person who designs flags.

West Point - The United States Military Academy (USMA) is a four-year federal service academy in West Point, New York. Sylvanus Thayer was the "Father of West Point." The Civil War divided America and is shown in these numbers from West Point graduates. 39 graduates who came from southern states fought for the North, and 32 graduates who came from the north fought for the confederacy.

Notable Confederate graduates: Confederate president Jefferson Davis, General Robert E. Lee and several of his relatives, James Longstreet, Stonewall Jackson, J.E.B. Stuart, etc. Notable graduates fighting for the Union are; Ulysses S. Grant, Philip Sheridan, William Tecumseh Sherman, Abner Doubleday, George Cook, etc. 259 graduates fought for the Confederacy, and 638 fought for the Union.

Yankee - Originally a nickname for people from New England, now applied to anyone from the United States. Even before the American Revolutionary War, the term Yankee was used by the British to refer, derisively, to the American colonists. During the Civil War, American southerners called all northerners Yankees. After the Civil War it is used to refer to any American.

Catharine Ziegler - was born in Germany in 1740. She is the mother of Barbara Fritchie. She had 10 children and Barbara was number five.

BIBLIOGRAPHY

The **Bible**. Revised Standard Version.

Census Reports from Frederick, Maryland.

Dall, Caroline H. *Barbara Fritchie, a Study.* 1892, page 38.

Douglas, Henry Kyd. *I Rode With Stonewall.* The war experiences of the youngest member of Jackson's staff. University of North Carolina Press. (Based on the 1886 version with many omissions and additions). 1940.

Engelbrecht, Jacob - From Frederick, Maryland, wrote in many *personal diaries* which historians have valued as a good record of the local history. In Frederick. The original diaries can be viewed at the history center. They were copied into 2 volumes which are for sale.

Jones, George O., and McVean, Norman S., and others compiled *History of Lincoln, Oneida and Vilas Counties, Wisconsin.* Published by H. C. Cooper, Jr. & Co., 1924.

Krom, Richard G. *The 1st MN Second to None.* p. 652 about the 8th Minnesota Regiment in Murfreesboro. 2010.

Official Records of the Rebellion. A Collection. Page 601 of Vol 19, Pt. 2.

Ryan, Joe. *"The Thomas Stonewall Jackson and Reverend Dr. John B. Ross Connection Revisited."* Article online.

Schaib, J. Thomas. *The History of Western Maryland; The History of Allegany County Maryland.* 1882.

Southern Historical Society, Virginia Historical Society. *Southern Historical Society Papers.* 52 volumes. Publisher: Richmond, Virginia Historical Society 1876-1959.

Thayer, Edna Louise. *The Spirit of Adventurous Albert Augustus (Gus) Thayer.* Poem. September, 2019.

Thayer, Tamara Louise. *The Veteran's Poppy.* Poem. April, 2019.

Thayer, Tamara Louise. *The Flag a Symbol of Patriotism.* Poem. 2019.

The Biographical Annals of Lancaster County, Pennsylvania: containing biographical and genealogical sketches of prominent and representative citizens and of many of the early settlers. Chicago: J.H. Beers & Co., 1903.

Whittier, John Greenleaf. *Barbara Freitchie.* Poem. 1863.

Interviews:
    Tasa, Barbara. third great-granddaughter of Barbara Fritchie.

    Thayer, Dave. third great-grandson of Barbara Fritchie.

    Wright, Susie. third great-granddaughter of Barbara Fritchie.

    The Frederick, Maryland; historians, Resource librarians staffed in the Maryland Room in the Frederick library, numerous museum staff at all of the museums in Frederick.

    Barbara Fritchie Restaurant previous owner, a Mount Olivet employee, pastor and historians from Barbara Fritchie's church on two different inquiries, and tour guides.

Newspapers and Magazine:
Baltimore Sun
    Engelbrecht, Jacob. "Letter to the editor." 24 April, 1875.

Confederate Veteran Magazine
    By Confederate Southern Memorial Association (U.S.) Sons of Confederate Veterans (Organization); United Confederate Veterans; United Daughters of the Confederacy. "Barbara Frietchie Revised." 1893.

    J. William Jones. "The Barbara Fritchie Myth". Volume 8, Pages 113–114. 1900.

Frederick News-Post

New York Times

A Correspondent of the Washington Star. "Barbara Fritchie Again."
Page 4. April 17, 1869.

An Ex-Confederate. "Barbara Fritchie Again." Page 9. April 15, 1875.

Reprinted from the Frederick Examiner. "The Demolition of the Home of
Barbara Fritchie." Page 3. May 16, 1869.

Reno, Jesse W. "The Real Barbara Frietchie" Page 18. Oct. 29, 1899.

Tyler, Samuel. "Barbara Fritchie." Page 8. April 26, 1875.

Whittier, John G. "Barbara Fritchie Once More - Letter from Whittier."
Page 2. February 25, 1869.

Terril Record

unknown author. Article on George Washington's visit. February 22, 1934.

The Century

Whittier, John G. "Letter to the editor." June 10th, 1886.

The News, Frederick, Maryland,

Unknown author. Article on George Washington's visit. October 8, 1949.

The San Francisco Bulletin

An Ex-Confederate. "Letter to the editor." April 4, 1875.

The Washington Post

Valley News Echo

Unknown Author. "President Lincoln Visits Battlefields." Hagerstown,
MD. October, 1862.

Washington Star

Whittier, John G. "Barbara Fritchie Once More - Letter from Whittier."
February 23, 1869.

Quantrill, Mary A. "Barbara Fritchie. Who Waved the Flag at
Fredericksburg?" Page 2. February 15, 1869.

Tours as part of investigative research:

Barbara Fritchie Museum. 2016.

Barbara Fritchie Airbnb. 2019.

Catoctin Mountains. 2019.

Civil War Battle Fields. Toured numerous battle fields in several states.

Frederick Visitor Center. Barbara Fritchie Display and landmark resources.

Fredericktown Hessian Barracks, Frederick, Maryland.

German Reform Church. Frederick, Maryland. Toured 2016, 2019.

Tours of Frederick, Maryland. 2016, 2017, 2019.

Mary (Colburn) Thayer's cemetery. Minnesota.

Maryland Room, C. Burr Artz Public Library.

Maryland School for the Deaf, Frederick, Maryland.

Mount Olivet Cemetery, Frederick, Maryland.

Museum of Frederick County History, Frederick, Maryland.

National Museum of Civil War Medicine, Frederick, Maryland. 2019.

Oneida Community Mansion House. Oneida, New York. 2016.

Websites and Online Resources:

https://lccn.loc.gov/21012986
Abbott, Eleanor Dorff. [from old catalog] A sketch of Barbara Fritchie, Whittier's heroine; including points of interest in Frederick, Maryland, by Miss Eleanor D. Abbott. [Frederick, Md., Frederick News-post pub. co.] c1921.

ancestry.com

civilwarhome.com - Battles and Leaders of the Civil War. n.d.

founders.archives.gov - Containing several letters from George Washington to Sally Cary Fairfax. n.d.

U.S. DEPARTMENT OF HEALTH AND HUMAN SERVICES Centers for Disease Control and Prevention, National Center for Health Statistics, National Vital Statistics System. online records. n.d.

A LESSON LEARNED FOR HISTORIANS, GENEALOGISTS, AND NEWSPAPER REPORTERS

The Authors Point of View

It is my practice when I research my genealogy or other historical events to not "assume" anything, and certainly not to fill in missing time periods with my guesses unless it is properly noted as such. I recommend to students, reporters, and any historical researchers in general that when doing research, one needs to gather as many resources as possible and double-check their reliability. I do this by initially putting the sources in the following categories; primary sources, secondary sources, and hearsay. When one finds an eyewitness account, one needs to look further into their biases and how much time has passed since the incident on which they are reporting. For example, two reporters could both be eyewitnesses to something that happened today. The eyewitness account may be reported in tomorrow's paper as two totally different perspectives or even look like two separate events. Here is a short list of resources I find and how I personally categorize them:

Primary sources:
Birth Certificates
Marriage Certificates
Divorce Decrees
Death Certificates
Court and Legal Records
Land and Probate Records
Wills
Obituaries
Church Records
Cemetery Records

Secondary Sources:
Family Bibles
Newspaper Articles
Yearbooks
Family Trees
Historical Societies
Census Reports
Town Directories
Local Museums
Eye Witnesses (depending if biased)
Family Scrapbooks (of genealogy records)
.gov or .mil Websites
.edu Websites - while some are reliable check for author's intent and credibility

Hearsay:
Blogs
Diaries or Journals
A 3rd Hand Account
Wikipedia
Political Sites - biased and used to sway public opinion
.com.co Websites
Any information that one "hears about," that needs further documentation to verify it, is considered just hearsay. This initial information can be useful in pointing one into the right direction to research and find a primary source or secondary source so it can be verified.

We cannot rewrite the past with our modern day speculations of a historical event.

CLASSROOM/BOOK CLUB DISCUSSION QUESTIONS

1. Was there a way Barbara could have freed slaves? What were some ways to free people who were slaves, and what were the consequences for each?

2. Would you have sacrificed your life for your flag?

3. What do you think were casualties of the Civil War? How was it different for the North vs the casualties for the South?

4. Do you believe Barbara waved the flag? Why or Why not?

5. Do you think Mary Quantrill also waved the flag, or was her incident made up to debunk Barbara's story?

6. Why was Frederick, Maryland, "The Crossroads" of the Civil War?

7. What lessons do you think historians can learn from the Barbara Fritchie story about preserving history?

8. How can you show your patriotism?

9. Write a 1-2 page story about Americanism and submit it to my website. One winner each year on Flag Day, June 14th, will receive a free book and a certificate.

10. How can we support our veterans?

11. How can Americans renew their pride in the flag of the USA?

12. Based on what you've read in this book, what is a lesson learned for genealogists?

www.tamarathayerbooks.org

CHECKING YOUR VEXILLOLOGY ARE YOU A VEXILLOLOGIST?

1. What color is the very first stripe on the top of the first official U.S. Flag?

2. What part of the flag is referred to as the Union?

3. How many points do the stars have on our current flag? Did they always have the same number of points?

4. How many stripes are there, and what do they represent?

5. How many stripes are red? How many stripes are white?

6. Was there always the same number of stripes?

7. There is only one official flag of the United States that doesn't need to be lowered at half mast on special occasions when all the rest are required to be. Where is that flag located?

8. How many stars were on the flag that Barbara Fritchie waved at Stonewall's men?

9. How many stars were on the flag raised at Iwo Jima?

10. When was the American Flag raised at "ground zero" in New York for the first time by three fireman?

Answers to the Vexillology questions

1. Red
2. The blue area
3. 5, no the first flag had 6 and there wasn't any regulation on how many our stars should have until 1912.
4. 13 for the 13 colonies
5. 7 Red, 6 white
6. No, there was 15 on the Star Spangled Banner Flag which was used from 1795-1818.
7. On the moon
8. 34
9. 48
10. On 9-11-01

★ ABOUT THE AUTHOR ★

Tamara Thayer's debut book, *A Country Doctor Goes to War*, was the winner of ten book awards. The moving story of her own grandfather Dr. Ellsworth Thayer's life was portrayed in this non-fiction biography.

Tamara is an ASL interpreter, public speaker, and a genealogist. If you are interested in having her speak on her books or a variety of topics, contact her on the website below.

She lives in Minnesota and enjoys time with her family, discovering genealogy, or researching other historical information for her next books. Her life adventures and love of travel have brought her to the side of an active volcano while taking pictures up close of hot lava, parasailing, diving down in a shark cage to see sharks up-close, snorkeling the Great Barrier Reef, touring European castles, and kissing the blarney stone for good luck. These daring adventures you may read about in one of her next books.

Books by Tamara Thayer
www.tamarathayerbooks.org

A Country Doctor Goes to War

The Mystery of Barbara Fritchie
A True Patiot